TRAIL
BLAZERS

SCIENTISTS

WHO DARED TO BE DIFFERENT

THE DANIEL GIRAUD ELLIOT MEDAL

TIME

EMILY HOLLAND

ARCTURUS

ARCTURUS

This edition published in 2020 by Arcturus Publishing Limited
26/27 Bickels Yard, 151–153 Bermondsey Street,
London SE1 3HA

Author: Emily Holland
Illustrator: Salini Perera
Designer: Dani Leigh
Editor: Donna Gregory
Art Direction: Jessica Holliland
Editorial Manager: Joe Harris

ISBN: 978-1-83857-601-1
CH007336NT
Supplier 29, Date 0520, Print run 9527

Printed in China

CONTENTS

INTRODUCTION

Throughout history, scientists have used their brilliance, insight, and imagination to improve the quality of our lives. They have reduced our chances of suffering from serious diseases, revolutionized our understanding of the planet on which we live, and flown into the unknown to explore the Universe. Even more strikingly, some scientists have made achievements of this sort in the face of extraordinary—even seemingly unsurmountable—challenges.

Here, we take a tour of some of the world's most courageous and resilient trailblazers in the field of science. These are people whose social status, gender, mental or physical health, or unusual ways of thinking might easily have prevented them from achieving anything significant in their lives—but whose determination, passion, courage, and hard work mean they have made spectacular discoveries in areas such as medicine, geology, nuclear physics, and astrophysics.

It is hard to imagine how **STEPHEN HAWKING**, who at the age of only 21 was diagnosed with ALS —a condition that quickly robbed him of his power of speech and movement —could have challenged previous understanding of the structure of the Universe for the better, through his study of black holes and string theory. Stephen defied his own

KATHERINE JOHNSON
PAGE 111

medical prognosis as well as the greatest minds in physics with his ground-breaking work. In the USA in the late 1800s, young **SUSAN LAFLESCHE** vowed to become the first female Native American doctor, at a time when few women in her community worked, let alone dreamed of a career in medicine. Despite her own lifelong illnesses, Susan worked tirelessly to improve the health of her people, as well as fighting for their civil and human rights and was the first person to educate Native Americans on the damage caused by alcohol. In 1963 the race to send women into space was won by the USSR, when it selected young **VALENTINA TERESHKOVA** from her humble background to be the first ever female space pilot. Valentina's childhood and adolescence had been spent helping her poverty-stricken, widowed mother feed and clothe the family, while still determined to realize her dream of becoming a cosmonaut—parachuting her way into and out of space!

STEPHEN HAWKING
PAGE 72

Meanwhile, the American **TEMPLE GRANDIN**, who was born severely autistic, has used her unique mind to understand the physical needs and responses of the animals she grew up with in Arizona, not only becoming a hugely successful animal psychologist, but a leading advocate of autism as a "gift" and not a "disability." Though all her life she has found relating to the humans around her very difficult, her special empathy with animals is undoubtedly a result of her autism.

In Poland in the 1800s, MARIE CURIE overcame depression and financial hardship—and the then-common belief that women should not be educated beyond school—to discover two vital elements for inclusion in the Periodic Table and make significant breakthroughs in X-ray technology—thus saving the lives of many people then and in the future. In wartime Britain, ROSALIND FRANKLIN fought the prejudice against women in her field of the early twentieth century to tirelessly experiment with DNA and X-ray crystallography. In doing so, she progressed the study of genetics and medical technology, resulting in quicker and more accurate diagnosis of serious illness—making the difference between life and death for many people.

The study of the stars and the religious beliefs surrounding "heaven" would still be trapped in time had GALILEO GALILEI not bravely stood by his theories on heliocentrism—defying the Church and suffering imprisonment in the process. And the lives of many blind, budding mathematicians would be very different now without the resourcefulness of American ABRAHAM NEMETH, himself blind from birth, who refused to accept that as a visually impaired person he could not teach mathematics at a high level. Instead he invented his own version of Braille, specifically for the study of calculus and equations—enabling many like him to succeed in their chosen career.

MARY ANNING's amazing childhood discoveries along the Jurassic Coast provided her impoverished family with an income as well as the scientific community with one of its sharpest paleontological minds, while MARIE THARP's determination to reveal the secrets of the ocean floor and Earth's crust, despite being a woman in a man's world.

The sixteen formidable scientists in this book faced challenges that undoubtedly made their lives more difficult. For some, their "disadvantages" were arguably vital to their success, while others were only inspired to work harder to achieve their goals by what was seen to hold them back. What is undeniably true is that without these trailblazers, we would lack much of the knowledge that has advanced our medical treatment and scientific understanding of the world in all its extraordinary glory.

CHIEN-SHIUNG WU
PAGE 80

GEERAT VERMEIJ
PAGE 50

"I AM DIFFERENT, NOT LESS."
TEMPLE GRANDIN

ALBERT EINSTEIN

EARLY LIFE

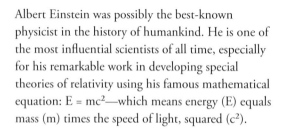

Albert Einstein was possibly the best-known physicist in the history of humankind. He is one of the most influential scientists of all time, especially for his remarkable work in developing special theories of relativity using his famous mathematical equation: $E = mc^2$—which means energy (E) equals mass (m) times the speed of light, squared (c^2).

Albert was born on March 14, 1879, in Württemberg, Germany. He was the first of two children born to middle-class Jewish parents, Hermann and Pauline Einstein. Albert's father Hermann was a feather-bed salesman, who later ran an electrochemical factory. Albert's only sibling, Maria—known as Maja—was born two years after Albert in 1881.

It has long been thought that Albert had significant learning difficulties in his younger years. His early speech problems, social awkwardness, and the eccentric lectures he later gave to students have led some modern experts to argue that he had Asperger Syndrome, a form of autism. Along with his difficulty communicating, Albert would obsessively fixate on things, and use unconventional methods to solve problems. It is thought that some

people with autism can also have a particular talent for understanding complicated concepts, such as mathematics, music, physics, and computer coding. Many believe that Albert also had a condition called "dyscalculia"—a mathematical learning disorder that enabled him to see numbers and formulas differently.

Albert wrote of two "wonders" that deeply affected his childhood. The first wonder came when he was 5 years old and saw how a compass worked for the first time. He was fascinated by the "invisible forces" that affected how the needle swung—this would lead to a lifelong curiosity for investigating invisible forces. The second of Albert's wonders came when he was 12 years old and found a book on geometry that sealed his love of science, and which he called his "sacred little geometry book."

At the same age, Albert became very interested in religion. He even wrote songs praising God and sang them on his way to school. However, it wasn't long before his love for and belief in science got in the way of his religious beliefs, challenging the idea of God in his mind.

"LIFE IS LIKE RIDING A BICYCLE. TO KEEP YOUR BALANCE YOU MUST KEEP MOVING."

THE REBEL WITH RADICAL IDEAS

Albert's secondary-school education was at the Luitpold Gymnasium, where the strict learning methods did not suit either his unconventional brain or his creativity. He didn't fit in, and one teacher even told him that he would never amount to anything. If it hadn't been for Max Talmud, a family friend, who became Albert's tutor in mathematics and philosophy, his scientific ability might have been permanently hidden. Talmud gave him a children's science book and its description of moving alongside electricity as it surged through a telegraph wire inspired Albert, who became gripped by the thought of what a light beam would look like if he were to run alongside it in the same way. It was a life-changing moment for him and he wrote his first scientific paper shortly afterward.

While he was at high school, Albert's parents moved to Italy due to the collapse of his father's business. Left behind in Munich to finish his education, the young Albert was very unhappy. He dreaded turning 16, when he would be made to go into military service. Desperate, he ran away to join his parents in Milan, arriving on their doorstep a high-school dropout and a "draft dodger."

Things changed for the better when he applied to the prestigious Swiss Institute of Technology in Zurich and was offered a place, providing he passed its hard entrance exam. First, Albert went to a special high school in Aarau, Switzerland, graduating in 1886 with exceptional mathematics and physics scores, which assured him a place at the Institute in Zurich. It was around this time that he met his first wife, Mileva Marić.

While he was at the institute in Zurich, Albert's "difficult" personality again caused problems. He often missed classes, which did not impress his teachers, who refused to recommend him. When he graduated in 1900 and applied for more academic positions, he was turned down every time. Meanwhile, his parents disapproved of his relationship with Marić on religious grounds and by 1902 he was in crisis again, forced to take positions tutoring children—until late that year, when accepted a job as a clerk in a patent office in Bern. At this time, his dying father finally gave him his blessing to marry Marić. Now that he was employed and about to settle down, Albert's passion for science burned bright again.

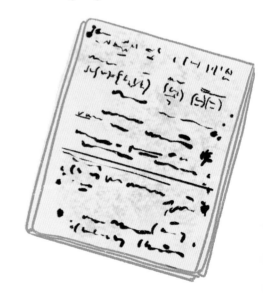

GREAT ACHIEVEMENTS

In the early 1900s, Albert's thoughts returned to the vision he'd had as a boy: What would happen if he raced alongside a light beam? While in Zurich, he had studied the nature of light, and discovered a previously unknown fact—that the speed of light stays the same no matter how fast one moves. This went against previously held beliefs and led Albert to come up with the principle of "relativity"—that "the speed of light is constant in any constantly moving frame."

During 1905—known as Albert's "miracle year"—he published four papers in a highly regarded scientific journal, *Annalen der Physik*, each of which would change the course of modern physics. In the same year he wrote a paper for his Ph.D. But Albert's 1905 papers were ignored by the scientific community until they came to the attention of one of the most influential physicists of his generation, Max Planck, who'd discovered "quantum theory." With Planck's endorsement, Albert's theories were gradually accepted, and he was invited to give lectures and offered many prestigious roles at universities all over the world.

At the end of 1915, Albert finally completed his "general theory of relativity," which he considered to be his masterpiece. When his theories were scientifically tested and proved correct, the results made newspaper headlines all over the world. In 1921, he embarked on the first of many world tours to speak about his work. He was hugely influential in the new science of cosmology, and came up with mathematical models for how the Universe both expands and shrinks.

In the early 1930s, the Nazis were gathering power in Germany. They branded Albert's theories "Jewish physics"—even burning his books to show their contempt for him. Fearing for his life, Albert left Germany forever in 1932, and settled successfully as a professor at Princeton University in the USA.

Toward the end of the 1930s, scientists began working on the atomic bomb, and by 1939 it had been proven that vast amounts of energy could be unleashed by the splitting of the uranium atom. This principle had previously been shown in Albert's famous equation, $E=mc^2$. This led to an elite group of scientists working on "the Manhattan Project" and developing the first atomic bomb, which was dropped over Japan in 1945. When he realized the destruction nuclear technology could cause, Albert called for worldwide controls on its use.

LEGACY

Albert Einstein died on April 18, 1955, at the age of 76, having spectacularly defied the school teacher who told him he would not amount to anything. As with many whose unusual brains have produced spectacular work, he made the challenges he faced in education and society work *for* and not against him. His experiments and study on the development of the atomic bomb changed the course of history and the way that modern warfare is fought. As part of the Manhattan Project he was instrumental in triggering the "Nuclear Age," something he was both proud and fearful of, following the dropping of the atomic bomb on Hiroshima and Nagasaki.

In Albert's contribution to mathematics and physics, and his now famous theory of relativity—$E=mc^2$—he exposed the underlying principle of the Big Bang, and our existence as human beings, and undoubtedly influenced Professor Stephen Hawking, who progressed Albert's ideas as well as coming up with his own in this area of science. Albert made more significant advances in the scientific field of cosmology, aiming for one big theory that would tie all physics theories together. Since his death, scientists have continued the work Albert started on higher dimensions and even time travel.

Though toward the end of his life Albert became increasingly isolated and felt he was not keeping up with modern science, he is widely believed to have been way ahead of his

time. In 1921, he won a Nobel Prize for Physics for his work on the photoelectric effect, and his many original ideas continue to inspire the scientists who have come after him, building on his work to win their own Nobel Prizes—including one for the discovery of gravitational waves. Along with these tributes, new generations of space satellites have continued to validate his work.

After his death, Albert's brain was removed and preserved in the hope that neuroscientists of the future would be able to discover what made him such a genius. Robert Oppenheimer, the lead scientist of the Manhattan Project, gave a memorial lecture celebrating Albert Einstein and his work, summing him up as "almost wholly without sophistication and wholly without worldliness … There was always with him a wonderful purity, at once childlike and profoundly stubborn."

ROSALIND FRANKLIN

SPORTY SCHOLAR

Rosalind Elsie Franklin was an English chemist whose scientific research has made a huge contribution to the world's understanding of the molecular structures of DNA, viruses, coal, and graphite, but it is only since her death in 1958 that her great achievements have been properly recognized.

Rosalind was born on July 25, 1920, in Notting Hill, London. She was the elder daughter and the second of five children in a wealthy and influential British-Jewish family. Her father, Ellis Arthur Franklin, was a merchant banker who was also actively involved with London's Working Men's College, where he taught subjects including electricity, magnetism, and the history of the World War I in the evenings, later became the college's vice-principal. Both he and Rosalind's mother, Muriel Waley, later helped settle Jewish refugee children from Europe who had escaped the Nazis in World War II, taking two of those children into their family home. Rosalind's aunt, Helen Caroline Franklin (known in the family as "Mamie"), was active in trade union organization and was very supportive of the women's suffragette movement. Rosalind's great uncle, Herbert Samuel,

was made Home Secretary in 1916 and the first observant Jewish man to be a member of the British Government.

Rosalind was a gifted all-round student from an early age. This became obvious when, aged 6, she and her brother Roland joined a private day school in West London. Rosalind was so eager to learn that her aunt Mamie described her as "alarmingly clever—she spends all her time doing arithmetic for pleasure." Rosalind was also a sporty child, and she particularly loved cricket and hockey.

When she was 9, Rosalind went to the Lindores School for Young Ladies, a boarding school near the coast in Sussex, where her family thought the sea air would be good for her delicate health. Then, at the age of 11, she entered St. Paul's Girls' School in West London—at the time one of the few girls' schools that taught physics and chemistry. Here, Rosalind excelled, not only in science and mathematics but in sport, Latin, German, and French—a language she would later find very useful in her career. She worked hard and came top in all her subjects except music, in which she was said to be tone deaf.

CHEMISTRY, COAL & DNA

"MY METHOD OF THOUGHT AND REASONING IS INFLUENCED BY A SCIENTIFIC TRAINING—IF THAT WERE NOT SO MY SCIENTIFIC TRAINING WILL HAVE BEEN A WASTE AND A FAILURE."

In 1938, at the age of 18, Rosalind won a scholarship to study chemistry for her Natural Sciences degree at Newnham College, part of Cambridge University. She got such outstanding results in her final exams that in 1941 she was awarded a rare research post in the Laboratory of Physical Chemical at Cambridge. Though always eager to learn, Rosalind became a little frustrated by her tutor there, a man called Ronald Norrish, who was known for his difficult personality. She felt she was not receiving the guidance from him that she needed, and a year later, in the middle of World War II, Rosalind resigned from Norrish's lab. Having been approved under the National Service Act she took a job as an assistant research officer for the British Coal Utilisation Association (BCUA), based in Kingston-upon-Thames near London. Here she studied the chemical properties and density of coal to judge its use as a fuel and its importance in the production of gas masks. Her work was of huge significance to the war effort, and it contributed to the Ph.D. thesis on the physical chemistry of coal that Rosalind earned from Cambridge in 1945. Along with her research work during 1942 to 1945, Rosalind volunteered as an air-raid warden, checking on the welfare of people during air raids.

With the war coming to an end in 1945, Rosalind began looking for work as a chemist. At a conference in the autumn of 1946, she was introduced to Marcel Mathieu, director of the national scientific research institute for the French government. Through her involvement with Marcel Mathieu, Rosalind was asked in 1947 to join a scientific laboratory in Paris as one of fifteen researchers working for the professor Jacques Mering, whose special interest was in X-ray photography. This was to be a life-changing role for Rosalind. Jacques Mering taught her the practical ways of how to apply X-ray photography to various substances, and she was soon fascinated by the study of X-ray crystallography, which is taking images of the atoms or molecules that make up crystals. Rosalind's research into X-rays was to be the first step in her incredible findings about DNA, the genetic code that makes all of us living creatures who we are.

PHOTO 51

In 1951, following her work in Paris, Rosalind took up a post at King's College, London, as a research associate in the Medical Research Council's Biophysics Unit, at the request of scientist John Randall, who was impressed by her work in Paris. Randall asked her to work on DNA strands, along with two other scientists: Maurice Wilkins, a molecular biologist, and Raymond Gosling, an assistant researcher. Despite a difficult relationship with Wilkins, Rosalind worked hard to bring her knowledge of both physical chemistry and X-ray diffraction (light waves bending around or through small openings) to study and analyze the structure of DNA. For this she used a specially focused X-ray tube and a camera she adapted herself for her purposes. Rosalind, Maurice Wilkins, and Raymond Gosling continued to work together using their special techniques on X-ray pictures of DNA and came up with varying results. Rosalind was convinced that they were missing something important about structure of DNA and was determined to discover what that was.

Eventually, by taking her now-famous X-ray image known as "Photo 51"—which has been described as "amongst the most beautiful X-ray photographs of any substance ever taken"—Rosalind hit on the groundbreaking information needed for molecular biologists James Watson and Francis Crick to discover the "double helix" model—the two twisted strands of DNA. This discovery was an amazing breakthrough in modern medical research and treatment, but at the time, Rosalind Franklin's vital contribution was somewhat overlooked.

In the 1950s, after finishing her work on DNA at King's College, Rosalind was funded by the British Agricultural Research Council to work at Birkbeck College, where she led pioneering research into the molecular structures of viruses, working alongside her team member Aaron Klug. Again using X-ray crystallography, Rosalind studied the structure of the tobacco mosaic virus (TMV) and the polio virus, making more important discoveries about DNA and viruses, and adding greatly to the important research being done on the polio virus at the time.

Franklin &
Gosling
Sodium
Thymonucleate
Type B

"SCIENCE, FOR ME, GIVES A PARTIAL EXPLANATION OF LIFE. IN SO FAR AS IT GOES, IT IS BASED ON FACT, EXPERIENCE AND EXPERIMENT."

RECOGNITION AT LAST

Rosalind Franklin died in 1958, aged 37, from ovarian cancer, having made hugely important contributions to three different fields of science in her lifetime. Despite not being given due credit for her work at the time, she is now known to have had a huge impact on our scientific knowledge of the structure of both viruses and DNA. Her research and experiments have led to our better understanding of illness and disease and to the continued study of genetic structures, and have enabled scientists to develop better treatments and medicines and given us all a better length and quality of life.

As a role model, Rosalind has been crucial to the crusade to encourage more women to embark on careers in the still male-dominated field of science. In the world of stem cell technology in particular, her discoveries have been held up as an example of the equal status woman have when it comes to the advancement of research. She is an inspiration to many women scientists, because of and not despite her reported stubborn and "difficult" personality. In the prime of her career she endured not only sexism, but anti-Semitism because of her Jewish faith. Her resolute determination to continue enabled significant advancements in healthcare.

She didn't live long enough to win a Nobel Prize for her work on the structure of DNA. Instead, in 1962, four years after her death, the prize was awarded to Francis Crick, Maurice Wilkins, and James Watson. In 1982, Aaron Klug, who assisted Rosalind in the pioneering research she led on the structure of viruses at Birkbeck College, was awarded a Nobel Prize for the research he carried on after her death. However, Rosalind has since been rightfully widely recognized by the global scientific community for her outstanding achievements. Along with the likes of King's College London and Newnham College in Cambridge naming their residences and laboratories after her, she's had computer software named after her. Grants and awards at the likes of the University of Groningen in Holland and London's Royal Society have been set up in her memory. And in 1997, a newly discovered asteroid was named 9241 Rosfranklin as a tribute to her. In 2003, the Royal Society of chemistry declared King's College London as a "National Historic Chemical Landmark." There is a plaque at the entrance of the main building, with the inscription:

Near this site Rosalind Franklin, Maurice Wilkins, Raymond Gosling, Alexander Stokes and Herbert Wilson performed experiments that led to the discovery of the structure of DNA. This work revolutionised our understanding of the chemistry behind life itself.

MARY ANNING

BEACH HISTORY

Mary Anning was a nineteenth-century fossil collector whose discovery of many important Jurassic dinosaur fossils played a vital part in the development of paleontology (the study of fossil animals) as a scientific subject in Britain.

Mary was born on May 21, 1799, in Lyme Regis, Dorset, England, close to what is now known as the Jurassic Coast. She was one of ten children born to Richard and Mary Moore Anning, though only Mary and her elder brother Joseph survived beyond childhood. When she was just a year old, Mary narrowly escaped being killed by an electrical lightning storm by sheltering under a tree. Local legend has it that this near-death incident was responsible for her high intelligence.

Mary's father was a cabinet maker and carpenter who collected fossils from beaches near the family home. Around 200 million years earlier, when the sea level had been much higher, and the region had been a sea bed, many dinosaur skeletons had been fossilized. As the sea level had fallen, these fossils could be found on the beach and above it, especially in the exposed rocky cliffs. As a child, Mary spent a lot of time with her father, helping him collect these fossils so that he could earn extra income by selling them to the growing tourist trade in the coastal town of Lyme Regis. One of the fossils found, a pretty coiled shell that was later identified as an ammonite (a type of mollusk that lived in the Jurassic period), was popular among visitors to the region. Mary's fascination with these strange and beautiful remains of a long-past age was born, and it was to prove a lifeline for her family and the start of her career in the discovery of ancient species.

Mary's formal education was limited to a few years in the local parish school, but even before the age of ten she had developed extraordinary skills in fossil collecting. In 1810, when she was eleven years old, Mary's father suffered a bout of consumption, weakening him and leading to a fatal cliff accident. Richard Anning died, leaving his family badly in debt. Mary's older brother Joseph was already serving an apprenticeship to an upholsterer, so it was down to Mary and her mother to provide for themselves, and fossil collecting became their main source of income. For Mary, the time she had spent trawling the beaches as a little girl with her father were about to start paying off.

DISCOVERING DINOSAURS

Astonishingly, Mary Anning's first major fossil find was at the age of 12, when, along with her brother Joseph, she found a complete dinosaur skeleton. Later, this skeleton was sent to the Natural History Museum in London and was there given its formal name of "ichthyosaur." Mary's groundbreaking find was hugely important to science and she was sharpening her skills. Through her keen observations of the Jurassic Coast she could predict where fossils might be found after storms. She was also skilled at removing the fossils without causing them any damage. Throughout this time Mary was often accompanied by her beloved dog Tray, who was a valuable assistant, once Mary had trained him to stand guard over interesting finds. Sadly, poor Tray was crushed by an unexpected cliff fall, which almost killed Mary too.

In 1823, Mary made perhaps her greatest discovery. She found the first complete *Plesiosaurus*—or "Near Lizard." This was a reptile that was 2.7 m (9 ft) long and lived in the sea. It had a long neck, short tail, small head, and four flippers that were pointed and shaped like paddles. Not only was it a rare find, it led to the creation of a new category in the dinosaur fossil field.

Mary taught herself geology, anatomy, paleontology, and scientific illustration, and despite her lack of formal training, her reputation was now growing in the scientific world. By the age of 24, she had her own shop in Lyme Regis, which was regularly visited by experts impressed by her understanding of fossils, and Mary began networking with scientists all over the world. She was by this time becoming a shrewd businesswoman, often conducting auctions with interested specialist museums for her unusual fossils.

In 1828, Mary found parts of a *Belemnosepia*, which is an invertebrate (an animal that does not have a backbone). This was the first invertebrate she'd discovered. The same year, she found a *Pterodactylus macronyx*—also known as "wing finger" and it was this find that brought her nationwide attention. She continued to make important discoveries, and in 1829 she found the fossil of a *Squaloraja*, a fish that was halfway between a ray and a shark. In 1830 she discovered a *Plesiosaurus macrocephalus*, which was bought for the then-huge sum of £200 by a collector called William Willoughby.

"THE CARPENTER'S DAUGHTER HAS **WON** A NAME FOR HERSELF, AND **DESERVED** TO WIN IT"
CHARLES DICKENS

REMEMBERING MARY

Mary Anning died from breast cancer in 1847, at the age of 47. She had never married, nor did she have any children. For somebody who had never received a formal education, and who was forced to become the family breadwinner at the age of 11, her achievements are extraordinary, gaining her deep respect from scientists all over the world.

Her geological discoveries are some of the most important ever made in the field. They have provided key information for our understanding of the history of Earth. She was an expert in many areas, including coprolites (fossilized dung). She also played a central role in improving the work of the trained experts working in the field of geology

in that period, influencing notable scientists such as William Buckland, Henry de la Beche, and William Conybeare. By the time of Mary's death, geology was firmly established as a science subject because of her work.

Mary's contribution was particularly significant in the 1800s, when there was not much in the way of evidence to challenge the firm religious beliefs about how the world had come to be. For centuries people thought that the world's human, animal, and geographical changes had come about from the story of creation as told in the Bible, such as the flood that caused Noah to gather pairs of animals on his ark. The incredible marine reptiles that Mary

"MARY ANNING [IS] PROBABLY THE MOST IMPORTANT UNSUNG (OR INADEQUATELY SUNG) COLLECTING FORCE IN THE HISTORY OF PALEONTOLOGY."
STEPHEN JAY GOULD

unearthed inspired the scientific community to look at different explanations for changes in the natural world.

Nine years before her death, in recognition of her great work, Mary was given an annuity—an annual payment—donated by members of the British Association for the Advancement of Science and the Geological Society of London. She was also made the first special member of the new Dorset County Museum. Her life has been commemorated by a stained-glass window in St. Michael's Church in Lyme Regis, near where Mary was born.

TEMPLE GRANDIN

A SENSITIVE GENIUS

Temple Grandin is a highly respected animal psychologist in the USA. As a very young child, she was diagnosed with autism and grew up to become a leading advocate of autistic communities, as well as a consultant on the humane treatment of animals, particularly livestock.

Temple Grandin was born on August 29, 1947, in Boston, Massachusetts to Richard Grandin and Eustacia Cutler. Her father, Richard, was a real-estate agent, while her mother, Eustacia, was a writer, singer, and actress. As an infant, Temple spoke little and did not like to be held or touched, often having temper tantrums. She was diagnosed with autism—a condition that affects the areas of the brain that control abstract thought, language, and social interaction. Very little was known about autism at the time, and medical experts initially thought it was caused by something occuring during pregnancy.

In the early 1950s, autistic children were thought to be developmentally disabled. Temple's parents were told by doctors that she was brain-damaged, and it was suggested that she should live in an institution where she could get long-term care. Eustacia did not want to take this advice, and instead took her to a neurologist, who suggested speech therapy and a home caregiver. Her mother made sure that she read stories to Temple daily, and placed her in the kinds of schools where well-trained and sympathetic teachers could make a difference. Despite this, her interactions with other children in school were difficult and she didn't speak until the age of 4.

As she grew older, Temple grew particularly fascinated by objects that spun or turned round. The whirring noise that a fan makes often caused her panic attacks. Doors, on the other hand, were soothing, as were animals. Her blossoming love of animals became clear the summer she spent on her aunt's cattle farm in Arizona when she was a teenager.

THE CATTLE QUEEN

Although tests proved that Temple had considerable issues with her short-term memory—meaning she could not follow written instructions or subjects such as algebra—her visual abilities were strong. As a teenager, she became aware that the distress she felt from a heightened sensitivity to sound is true for both autistic people and animals. It was while she was staying at her aunt's ranch at that time that she saw a "squeeze chute" being used by ranchers to calm a cow so that it could be vaccinated or branded. Intrigued, Temple designed a "squeeze machine" to relieve her own nervous tension, basing it on the chute she'd seen on the ranch. It was so effective that improved versions of her machine were later used not only in schools to soothe autistic children but also by autistic adults to comfort themselves.

Despite obstacles to learning at school, Temple went on to have great academic success. In 1970, she earned a degree in psychology from Franklin Pierce College, followed by a master's degree in Animal Science from Arizona State University, then a Ph.D. in Animal Science from the University of Illinois. She began working in the cattle industry, seeing first-hand the methods used to slaughter animals and how much stress and anxiety this caused for them. She then achieved her ambition, which was to design humane environments and facilities for livestock, such as cattle, who are reared for slaughter. She went on to work as a consultant for companies with large animal slaughterhouse

operations, advising them on ways of improving the quality of life of their cattle, and has campaigned widely for all animals to have a life free from anxiety and distress.

As a high-functioning autistic person, Temple Grandin's extreme sensitivity to detail and environmental change has been vital for her insight into the minds of cattle and domesticated animals. In regard to autism, she supports early intervention and teacher-training to give individual attention to each child's specific fixations— inspired by her own mother's efforts and results with her. She is also a champion of "neurodiversity"—arguing that autism should be seen as a gift rather than a disability, and that her work in the field of animal welfare would not have been possible without the insights and sensitivities that are a result of her autism.

ACHIEVEMENTS

Temple Grandin's remarkable work as an animal psychologist has earned her huge respect and status in the farming world. Her insights into the psychology of cattle in particular, and how the animals bred for slaughter respond to their treatment in captivity, led to the McDonald's fast-food chain hiring her as a consultant during a legal case over its treatment of the animals slaughtered for its meat products. Since the early 1990s, a large number of slaughterhouses in America have taken up her designs and innovations, and are now embracing her concern for animal welfare and complying with the humane-handling guidelines she laid out for the American Meat Institute.

As a high-achieving animal scientist Temple is living proof that autism can be harnessed for the good of society and industry, something that has been widely recognized in the USA, by both academics and the general public. In 2009, she was named a fellow of the American Society of Agricultural and Biological Engineers. She has also been given numerous special education, livestock industry, and animal-welfare group awards.

Along with her work in animal psychology, Temple Grandin is an influential ambassador for autism. With her strong belief that to be autistic is not to be disabled but to be gifted with a different kind of brain, she has campaigned throughout her life for this view to be accepted in the wider autistic community and among the medical professionals who help those with autism and their carers to manage their lives. She has spoken widely on this issue in the USA, for the Autism Society of America, including giving teachers and parents insights into appropriate methods of handling autistic children. She continues to tour many times a year to talk to audiences about autism and Asperger Syndrome, and uses every opportunity in the media to spread her message that autism should not be "cured" but instead should be accepted and celebrated. She has written multiple books on this subject, along with her writing on animal welfare.

Temple has also been a figure of fascination for psychologists, including Oliver Sacks, who wrote about her in his 1995 book *An Anthropologist on Mars*—its title refers to the isolation she and others like her feel in social situations. In 2010, American TV network HBO released a film entitled *Temple Grandin*, which was a drama—or biopic—about her life, and received 15 Emmy Award nominations, winning 5 of them. Temple is an inspirational example of the power of unconventional brains and the unique contribution they can make to the world—and to what can be achieved with belief and determination and hard work.

GALILEO GALILEI

A CURIOUS CHILD

Galileo Galilei was born on February 15, 1564, in Pisa, Italy, and was the oldest of six children, though only three of his siblings survived beyond infancy. His father was Vincenzo, a musical composer who was a famous lutenist, and his mother was Giulia. They were a close family of talented musicians, particularly Galileo's brother Michelangelo, who grew up to be a talented composer and lutenist, like their father. When Galileo was around 8 years old, his family moved to the city of Florence, and Galileo's formal education began at the age of 10, when he started school at the Camaldolese monastery in Vallombrosa—around 30 km (20 miles) away from Florence. Young Galileo had ambitions to become a priest when he grew up, but Vincenzo had other ideas. He wanted his son to one day pursue a career in medicine, which would provide a good income and a more secure financial future.

In 1581, when Galileo was 17 years old and had left the monastery school for the University of Pisa, he realized where his future vocation lay.

Watching a chandelier swinging unevenly—in large and small "arcs"—and yet still taking exactly the same amount of time to come back to its central position, inspired Galileo to conduct an experiment. Setting up two pendulums of the same length, he swung them in the same way that he'd seen the chandelier swinging—so that they had an uneven "sweep." Like the chandelier, both pendulums took the same time to complete one swing. They were synchronized. It was this, and a lecture on geometry that Galileo wandered into by accident at the university, that led him to decide on his true calling, which was in mathematics. Since he had already started studying Medicine at the University of Pisa, he had to persuade his father to allow him to transfer to Mathematics, with his secondary subject as Philosophy. Reluctantly, Vincenzo agreed and Galileo embarked on his new degree course. Meanwhile, his brother Michelangelo was proving irresponsible with money, which was a cause of tension in the family and something that would interrupt Galileo's education.

THE LITTLE BALANCE

> "YOU CANNOT TEACH A MAN ANYTHING; YOU CAN ONLY HELP HIM FIND IT WITHIN HIMSELF."

While studying at Pisa, Galileo intended to work toward an academic career teaching mathematics and philosophy with a focus on the ancient Greek philosopher Aristotle—who was the best known of the philosophers at the time and much discussed at the university. His plans were spoiled, however, when Michelangelo's health and financial difficulties meant the family did not have enough money for Galileo to finish his studies, and he left the University of Pisa early, in 1585, without having received a degree.

At 21 years old, Galileo was forced to lower his career expectations and concentrate on earning a living. He began giving private tuition in mathematics in Florence, while conducting scientific experiments in his spare time. It was during this period that he worked on "hydrostatics"—a study in the physics and characteristics of pressure in fluid, and wrote a lengthy paper on the subject, entitled La Bilancette—"The Little Balance." He also studied "motion"—the altered position of an object dependent on its surroundings in a specific period of time. At this time, these experiments and his paper started to bring him

recognition among science scholars, and though he continued to earn money through tuition, his reputation in mathematics and physics was growing.

In around 1589, Galileo was asked to become the head of Mathematics at the University of Pisa. There is a story that during his time here, he conducted an experiment which involved dropping objects of different weights from the top of the city's leaning tower. The results of this reportedly challenged the philosopher Aristotle's view that the speed of a falling object is directly related to how heavy it is. Galileo then lost faith in the teachings of Aristotle, and transferred it to the philosopher Archimedes instead, whose scientific findings were closer to his own. Galileo later secured himself a job at the University of Padua—again as head of mathematics. It was at the beginning of his time at Padua that Galileo's father died, and he had to step up as head of the family. Since his university income was not enough to cover all the expenses of the family and the care-taking of his younger brother Michelangelo, Galileo taught students in wealthy private schools to earn extra money.

WRITTEN IN THE STARS

It was in 1609, toward the end of his time at the University of Padua, that Galileo made his most groundbreaking scientific discoveries.

Having studied an early model of a telescope from the Netherlands, Galileo improved on it and built his own version. In 1610, using his new telescope, he discovered four new "stars" that were orbiting the planet Jupiter—identifying them as its four largest moons. Soon after this, he published a short paper laying out his findings and what he had observed about the moon's surface, and the many new stars he had discovered in the Milky Way. Galileo's paper on what was called "heliocentrism" confirmed the theories of another philosopher, Copernicus, that the Sun is the central star in the Universe and that Earth is a planet.

Galileo's discoveries turned him into something of a celebrity in Italy. Cosimo II, king at that time, made him official mathematician and philosopher to the ruling family of the Medicis, and that boosted his confidence enough to be able to publicly proclaim his great theories.

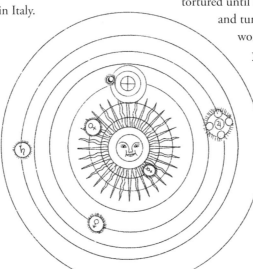

Once again, Galileo's observations contradicted the Aristotelian view of the Universe, which at the time was widely accepted by scientists. More importantly, in a country and time dominated by the Roman Catholic Church, Galileo's description of the moon's rugged surface went against the idea of heavenly perfection, and his account of the orbits of the stars challenged the belief that the heavens revolved around Earth. In 1616, Pope Paul V ordered Galileo to Rome and warned him against teaching his differing ideas.

Though over the years Galileo tried to add balance to his work to please the Church it wasn't enough, and in 1633, when he was nearly 70 years old, he was put on trial and summoned before the Roman Inquisition. He was found guilty of heresy—defiance of religious beliefs—and was tortured until he agreed to change his ways and turn his back on his scientific work. Galileo spent the last nine years of his life under a form of house arrest, at the palace of Ascanio Piccolomini, where he used the time to write a complete summary of his experiments on motion, which was his last great scientific work.

"IN QUESTIONS OF SCIENCE, THE AUTHORITY OF A THOUSAND IS NOT WORTH THE HUMBLE REASONING OF A SINGLE INDIVIDUAL."

THE FATHER OF MODERN SCIENCE

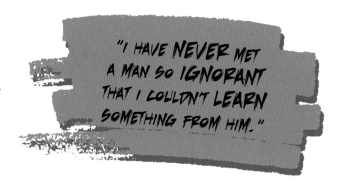

"I HAVE NEVER MET A MAN SO IGNORANT THAT I COULDN'T LEARN SOMETHING FROM HIM."

Galileo died on January 8, 1642, at the age of 78, from a fever. At the time of his death he was still considered a heretic by the Pope, so his funeral was modest. Though his family and friends, including the Duke of Tuscany, had wanted to bury him in the main part of the Basilica of Santa Croce in Florence, that was not allowed. Instead he was laid to rest in a small chapel until 1737, when his body was moved and reburied in its originally intended position.

Galileo Galilei was the first to properly study the planets using a telescope—at the time considered a truly "cutting-edge" piece of scientific equipment. His discovery that Earth revolved around the Sun—a fact that modern generations take for granted, led to future astrophysicists and scientists, such as Einstein and Hawking, producing their own groundbreaking theories in the field. His study and discovery of heliocentrism challenged the Church's power to control how the public perceived the landscape and the role of the Universe. It suited religious orders for people to believe that it was only God's mysterious forces that were shaping what was beyond Planet Earth. With the knowledge imparted by Galileo, the world began to wake up to a new way of thinking, and the scientific community, both in his lifetime and beyond, was empowered to make more spectacular discoveries, and continue to do so.

It was only in the twentieth century that the Church formally pardoned Galileo and acknowledged his extraordinary and accurate contribution to science, recognizing that he had a major part to play in the "scientific revolution."

Many things have been named after Galileo, including the "Galilean moons of Jupiter" and the *Galileo* spacecraft, Asteroid 697 Galilea. The International Year of Astronomy collector's coin features a picture of him and he has been paid tribute to in countless plays, novels, and movies depicting his life and works. He is hugely important in all our lives, not just educationally, through his great brain and astonishing experiments, but for the courage he showed in defending his radical findings, which transformed scientific thinking for all time and have led to his reputation as the "Father of Modern Science."

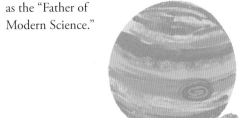

FAMILY LABORATORY

Born Maria Skłodowska in Warsaw, Poland on November 7, 1867, Marie was known in her family as "Manya." She was the fifth and youngest child of Bronisława and Władysław Skłodowski, who were both highly regarded teachers in Warsaw. Marie was taught to read and write from an early age and was a very intelligent child, with a real love of learning. Her parents came from families that had been active in trying to reclaim Poland's independence from Russia, losing a lot of their wealth in the process.

With little money coming in to the family, Marie's parents struggled to afford education for their children, and though her mother had a good job as headmistress of a respected boarding school, she had to give it up just before Marie was born. To bring more money in, the Skłodowskis took lodgers into their home, while her father Władysław continued to teach mathematics and physics, both subjects that Marie came to have a natural talent for. Because the State had forbidden laboratories in schools, Marie's father brought laboratory equipment home, and used it to teach Marie and her siblings basic physics and chemistry—it was then that Marie's love of the sciences was born.

When she was ten years old, Marie's mother died of tuberculosis—less than three years after her older sister Zofia had died of typhus. Young Marie was devastated. She had been brought up as a Catholic, but the deaths of her mother and sister made her strongly doubt her faith and she became an agnostic—she no longer believed in the existence of God.

In 1887, Marie attended a boarding school, followed by a "gymnasium" school, and from there she graduated in June 1883, at the age of 16, with a gold medal—the highest award for a school student. However, her family's pride in this achievement was dented by Marie collapsing and becoming ill shortly after she graduated. It was believed that she was suffering from severe depression and her anxious father sent her first to the countryside to live with relatives in order to recover, before she came back to Warsaw to live with him.

FIGHTING FOR AN EDUCATION

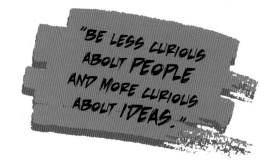

"BE LESS CURIOUS ABOUT PEOPLE AND MORE CURIOUS ABOUT IDEAS."

After having graduated from high school and recovering from her illness, Marie very much wanted to attend a university, but this wasn't something that women were allowed to do in Poland in the 1800s. University was thought only suitable for men. Determined to pursue further education anyway, Marie and her sister Bronisława found a place to study—a Polish university that was hidden from the state but that allowed women to learn. It was known as the "Flying" or "Floating" university. Bronisława's ambition was to then go to Paris and study medicine and though Marie longed to leave Poland and go to France too, there was simply not enough money for both sisters to be educated there. Instead, Marie stayed at home in Warsaw and worked as a home tutor and a governess to help fund Bronisława's study and life in Paris. Their plan was that as soon as she could afford to, Marie would then join her sister in France and attend the University of Paris.

At the start of 1890, Bronisława was some way through her medical training in Paris and had got married, while Marie was still struggling to save enough money for her tuition fees in France. It took her a year and a half to get the funds, and she was helped by her father, who by this time had got himself a well-paid job. In the meantime, Marie continued to educate herself. In between 1890 and 1891 she did her practical scientific training in a chemistry laboratory at the Museum of Industry and Agriculture near Warsaw's Old Town. The lab was run by her cousin, Jozef Boguski, who had been an assistant to the now well-known Russian chemist, Dmitri Mendeleev.

In late 1891, Marie finally left Poland for Paris, and for a short time lived with Bronisława and her husband before renting rooms in the Latin quarter of the city closer to the University of Paris, where she began studying physics, chemistry, and mathematics. She lived on little money, keeping herself warm during cold winters by wearing all the clothes she had. Marie was so focused on her studies and teaching in the evenings that she sometimes forgot to eat, but her hard work paid off. In 1893, she was awarded a degree in physics and began work with Professor Gabriel Lippman in his laboratory. All the while, she continued studying at the University of Paris and in 1894, with the help of a grant, she earned a second degree in mathematics.

SCIENCE IN A SHED

In 1894, having earned her two degrees, Marie met her future husband, Pierre Curie, a professor at the Municipal School of Industrial Physics and Chemistry in Paris. During the summer break of this year, Marie briefly returned to Warsaw to visit her family. Having earned her two degrees in Paris, she was hopeful she would now be able to work in her chosen field in Poland, but again she was refused a place at Krakow University because she was a woman. Pierre wrote to her, urging her to return to Paris where she could work toward her Ph.D.—the highest qualification awarded to a university student—and she agreed, returning to Paris where she was to begin working with Pierre in his laboratory.

In the laboratory—a converted shed next to the School of Physics and Chemistry in Paris—Marie began to research the invisible rays (such as those found in X-rays) given off by the chemical element uranium, which is a radioactive metal. The scientist Professor Henri Becquerel had recently discovered that these rays were able to pass through solid matter and that they caused air to conduct electricity. Marie was determined to find out what exactly was making these rays so powerful.

Using instruments that Pierre had invented, Marie measured the electrical currents found in air that had been bombarded with the uranium rays, looking for the different effects of these rays. She also examined a mineral called pitchblende for the same reason. In pitchblende, Marie found a large number of rays that could not be caused by uranium

alone but by something very radioactive that was only there in tiny quantities. Her search was now on to find out what this mysterious property was.

In 1898, after years of further experiments, Marie and Pierre found what they had been looking for—not one, but two previously undiscovered chemical elements: Polonium (named by Marie after her native Poland) and radium. This was a huge breakthrough in medical science and, because of it, Marie went on to develop the X-ray machine in time for its vital use during World War I, which changed the lives of thousands of the injured and unwell for the better. However, working so closely with poisonous elements would have a severe effect on Marie's own health.

"NOTHING IN LIFE IS TO BE FEARED. IT IS ONLY TO BE UNDERSTOOD."

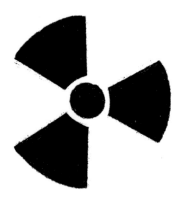

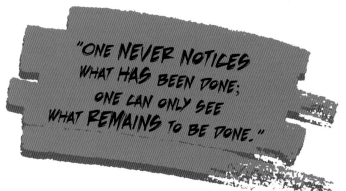

"ONE NEVER NOTICES WHAT HAS BEEN DONE; ONE CAN ONLY SEE WHAT REMAINS TO BE DONE."

INSPIRATIONAL WOMAN

Marie Curie died at the age of 67, in July 1934, from radiation poisoning—caused both by her experiments and by her work with X-ray machines. Even through her death, she threw light on scientific evaluation of the dangers of large doses of radiation. Today there are lots of safety measures to keep both scientists and patients from overexposure to radiation rays.

Her great work defied previously held ideas in physics and chemistry. She also challenged expectations by working at a time when women were not encouraged to educate themselves or have careers, let alone make groundbreaking scientific discoveries. She led the way for many women in the scientific field and beyond.

She was the first woman to win a Nobel Prize with her husband Pierre Curie and scientist Henri Bequerel in 1903, and the first person to win two Nobel Prizes when she was awarded the prize again, for Chemistry in 1911. The Curie symbol "Ci"—a unit of radioactivity—is named after Marie and Pierre Curie, and the chemical element with the atomic number 96 was named Curium. Added to this, three radioactive minerals are also named after the Curies: Curite, sklodowskite, and cuprosklowskite. Marie's eldest daughter Irene proudly followed in her mother's footsteps by working in the same scientific field, and herself won a Nobel Prize in Chemistry.

Marie has received many awards, and many degrees from universities across the world. In a 2009 survey carried out by New Scientist magazine she was voted the "most inspirational woman in science" and her name is included on the monument to the "X-ray and Radium Martyrs of All Nations," erected in Hamburg, Germany in 1936. Like Rosalind Franklin, Marie has an asteroid named after her, the 7000 Curie asteroid. There are countless places and institutions dedicated to her, including those that recognize her vital work in the progress of modern health and medicine. In Britain, Marie Curie Cancer Care was set up in 1948 to care for the terminally ill and the Curie Institute in Paris, which was founded by her in 1921, is still a major cancer research facility. In 2017, The Marie Curie Legacy Campaign was launched by the ESTRO Cancer Foundation—a global project to raise awareness of the benefits of radiotherapy and make it as widely available as possible to those in need all over the world.

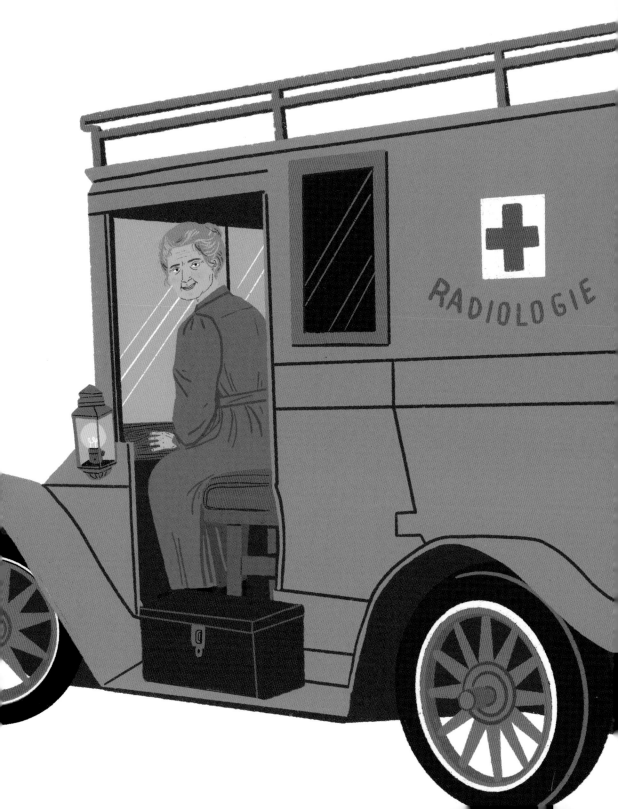

GEERAT VERMEIJ

THE LITTLE BEACHCOMBER

Geerat Vermeij—pronounced ver-may—was born on September 28, 1946, in the Netherlands. At birth, he was diagnosed with glaucoma—an eye condition that causes damage to the optic nerve—which meant he was unable to make out more than fuzzy shapes, and was completely blind by the age of 3. Nonetheless Geerat had a happy childhood. His mother and father were both keen nature lovers, and his father had been trained in arboriculture—which is the cultivation of trees and shrubs. As a small boy, Geerat loved to collect pine cones and leaves from the family garden or the grounds of the school he attended—along with rocks and stones from the local beach—learning to recognize these objects by feeling and smelling them.

Geerat attended the Dutch Prins Alexander Stichting Boarding School in Huis ter Heide, where he studied Braille and learned to love reading—though neither he nor his parents enjoyed being separated. At the time there were not many schools in Holland for blind children that didn't involve pupils living away from their families. Geerat's parents, who had been thinking of emigrating for

a while, looked for a place to move to where their son could have as normal a childhood as possible, and a schooling where he could live at home. They settled on New Jersey in the USA, where the policy on education for the blind was one of the most advanced in the world. Here, blind students were encouraged to attend regular schools and mix with non-visually impaired children. Having found the right environment for their son, the Vermeij family moved to America—and at the age of 10, Geerat started at a mainstream day school.

Arriving in New Jersey, Geerat was fascinated by the landscape, the different types of vegetation and the strange, noisy, sometimes poisonous, creatures that were found in and around his new home. One of his teachers had filled her classroom with shells she had brought from Florida, and it was these fossilized remains of mollusks and crustaceans that kick-started Geerat's scientific interest in marine science and paleobiology. With the help of his family, he read and investigated everything he could about sea life, biology, and general science, working toward his qualifications and his future career.

HOW SHELLS ARE FORMED

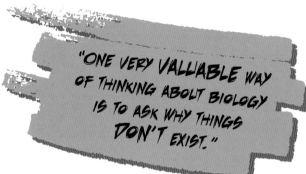

"ONE VERY VALUABLE WAY OF THINKING ABOUT BIOLOGY IS TO ASK WHY THINGS DON'T EXIST."

On leaving high school in New Jersey, Geerat studied at Princeton University, and graduated from there in 1968. Shortly afterward, he moved on to Yale University, where in 1971 he earned his Ph.D. in Biology and Geology. He then became a researcher at the University of Maryland College Park, where he received his first professorship. He went on to do marine biological research in Guam, the Philippines, the Galapagos Islands, Canada, Hawaii, and the Aleutian Islands. In the course of his career, he has taught students about paleobiology—the study of marine fossils—at all levels, including middle school, but settled at the University of California, where his research has focused on the Californian coast, as well as French Polynesia and New Zealand

Geerat's main interest in the fossilized shells he collects was to do with their function. He wanted to know how the shells worked for the creatures that built them, and how their shape reflected their

environment. He soon learned that the structure and shape of the shells originated from the predatory creatures against which they once had to defend themselves. Their shape was also useful for burrowing down into the sand and hiding from danger. As he studied them, Geerat learned not only about the shells themselves but also about the history of Earth and its animals over thousands of years. For him they were a window on a wider world, telling him and all of us about the history of life on Earth and how our planet and oceans have evolved over many thousands of years.

As he worked, examining the historical patterns of herbivores and the plants they ate, as well as organisms that bored into rocks, Geerat began to see the similarities between the evolving life and actions of these creatures and human life—including how both behave when they are under threat and what strategies they put in place to protect themselves. What is remarkable is that Geerat has done all of this brilliant, dedicated work without the ability to see. Instead he has read and researched with Braille, and used his heightened senses of smell and touch, feeling how shells have been formed and damaged and calculating the measurements and the power of the claws and jaws of the predators that attacked them as living creatures.

THE BLIND VISIONARY

During his remarkable career, Geerat Vermeij has developed an influential research project based upon the long-term evolutionary interaction between predators and their prey. In his work, he has effectively reinforced the Darwinian view of competition among species.

Using touch rather than sight as his guide, Geerat has made crucial discoveries about form and function in mollusk shells, and about the structure and arrangement of invertebrate reef communities. His studies of the animals of particular regions' geological periods has provided important evidence of the vital role of environment in evolution.

Geerat has written many dozens of scientific papers and four books, which include *Evolution and Escalation: An Ecological History of Life, A Natural History of Shells,* and his autobiography: *Privileged Hands: A Scientific Life.* He was also an editor for the journal *Evolution*—a magazine dedicated to the study of evolution. In 1992, Geerat was given a MacArthur Fellowship, a grant that is sometimes referred to as "the genius grant," and in 2002 he was awarded the Daniel Giraud Medal from the National Academy of Sciences. Not surprisingly, Geerat has a large and impressive collection of shells!

Among young scientists in his field, he is considered something of a hero whose blindness has not hindered his work and may even have improved it through his sharp senses of smell and touch. His message to anyone who wants to pursue a career in science is both modest and inspirational:

"Love your subject, be prepared to work hard, don't be discouraged by the occasional failure, be willing to take risks, get as much basic science and mathematics as you can take, and perhaps above all display a reasoned self-confidence without carrying a chip on your shoulder."

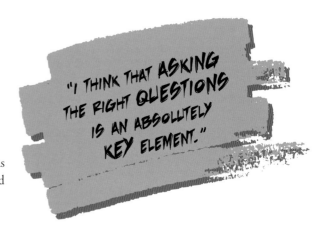

"I THINK THAT ASKING THE RIGHT QUESTIONS IS AN ABSOLUTELY KEY ELEMENT."

SUSAN LAFLESCHE PICOTTE

PLAINS LIFE

Susan was born in June 1865 on the Ohama Reservation—an area of land managed by the Native American Omaha Tribe, in eastern Nebraska in the USA—and was the youngest of four girls. She also had an older half-brother, Francis LaFlesche, who later became a well-known professor of ethnology, anthropology (both involve study of people and human relationships), and musicology (a study of music), focusing on the Native American Omaha and Osage cultures. Susan's parents were both of mixed race and had lived for periods of time beyond the borders of the reservation.

Susan's father, Joseph LaFlesche, known in the Omaha Tribe as "Iron Eye" was of Ponca (a mid-western Native American Tribe) as well as French Canadian origins. Though he was educated in St. Louis, he identified as Omaha and returned to its reservation as a young man where he was adopted by its leader "Chief Young Elk" in 1853. Joseph went on to become chief of the Omaha Tribe in 1855 and was keen to help his people achieve the same status and rights as all other US citizens.

Susan's mother, Mary Gale, was of mixed Omaha-Oto-Iowa heritage and she was the stepdaughter of a respected fur trader and statesman from Nebraska. Like Susan's father, Mary identified as Omaha, too. Though she understood French and English, she never spoke any other language than Omaha.

Growing up, Susan learned the traditions of her heritage, but her parents felt that certain Native American rituals would work against her among white people and so they didn't give her an Omaha name or the traditional Omahan tattoos across her forehead, and though Susan spoke Omaha with her parents, she was encouraged to speak English with her sisters.

A COMMUNITY VOCATION

As a child, Susan went to a white "mission" boarding school—where Native American children lived apart from their families and were taught the habits of white people, in the hopes of them blending in to white society in later life. After several years, Susan moved from this school to the Elizabeth Institute—a high school in New Jersey— where she stayed until she returned briefly to the Omaha Reservation to teach. In the early 1880s, aged 17, Susan left again for higher education at the Hampton Institute in Hampton, Virginia.

The Hampton Institute was a traditionally black college that also educated Native American

"I KNOW THAT I SHALL BE UNPOPULAR FOR A WHILE WITH MY PEOPLE ... BUT THIS IS NOTHING, JUST SO I CAN HELP THEM FOR THEIR OWN GOOD."

students. At the Hampton Institute, the girls learned "housewife" skills and the boys learned vocational—or career—skills. Here, Susan had her first brief romance with a young Sioux man, but she broke off their relationship before graduating. In 1886, when she left the Hampton Institute at 21, Susan was awarded the Demorest Prize—something only awarded to the graduating student who had gained the highest examination scores during their junior year. Although female Hampton graduates were encouraged to go on to teach or return to their reservations to become wives and mothers, Susan was intent on a career in medicine. The general view in society at the time was the women could be "healers," but it was not accepted that any woman, particularly a Native American, could go to medical school and become a doctor. Nevertheless, Susan applied for a place at the Women's Medical College of Pennsylvania (WMCP), one of the few medical schools on the East Coast for the education of women. Not only was she granted a place, she was given full financial support by the Women's National Indian Association (WNIA).

Susan had written to the WNIA, telling them that if she trained to be a doctor, she would enter the homes of her people not only to treat illness but also to teach them about hygiene. The WNIA were satisfied that Susan's ambitions matched their values. They paid for her medical school expenses and also funded her housing, her books, and other supplies. Susan was the first person to receive this state aid for her professional education in the USA. In return they asked her to remain single throughout her training and for several years afterward, so that she could focus on her career.

COMMUNITY DOCTOR

At medical school, Susan studied general medicine while doing internships (work placements) at teaching hospitals, returning home briefly once to take care of some of her Omaha family, who were sick from a measles outbreak. Even back at college, Susan regularly wrote home, using her medical knowledge to advise her people on how to treat illness. In 1889 at the age of 24, she graduated from the WMCP at the top of her class. Her achievements at college prompted the Connecticut Indian Association to ask her to become their ambassador and help them convince the white authorities that Native Americans would benefit from white medicine. In return, the Association helped Susan financially during her early years of work as a doctor.

Also in 1889, Susan was offered the job of government physician at the Omaha Agency Indian School, where she was responsible for teaching the students about cleanliness, along with keeping them well and healthy. During this time, she also cared for members of the wider Omaha community and was soon working 20-hour days, becoming responsible for over 1,200 people. She was not only their doctor, she also helped them with tasks such as writing letters and understanding official documents too.

Susan became a highly trusted member of the Omaha community. She made regular house calls, treating and educating patients with tuberculosis, cholera, dysentery, and the flu. Her work continued for years until 1892, when she became very ill and was bedridden for weeks. She had no choice but

to take time off to recover properly. Then in 1893, her mother became terminally ill, and Susan resigned from her job to take care of her.

By 1898, Susan had married Henry Picotte and they had two children. With Henry's support, she then returned to work, even though at the time married women were not expected to have jobs. Susan was determined, taking her children with her on house calls if necessary. As well as treating and preventing illness, she educated people on the dangers of drinking too much. Alcoholism was common in her community and encouraged by white people, who took advantage of addicts by persuading them to give up their land. For Susan, teaching Native Americans to respect and take care of themselves was vital, and she dedicated herself to helping both men and women achieve their rightful status as citizens of the USA.

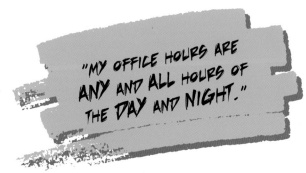

"MY OFFICE HOURS ARE ANY AND ALL HOURS OF THE DAY AND NIGHT."

A NOTABLE HEROINE

Susan LaFlesche Picotte died in 1915 from bone cancer, having suffered from chronic illness in later life. It is thought her dedication to her work took a great toll on her health. She had campaigned for a new hospital to be built on Walthill on her reservation, but by the time it was built she was too ill to run it. Today, inspired by Susan, that hospital serves as a drug and abuse treatment facility a cause her great-nephew, Dennis Farley, says she would have approved of. A school in western Omaha is also named after her and in 2018, a bust of her was erected in Sioux City.

In her lifetime, Susan did extraordinary work in healthcare and social reform for her community, serving more than 1,300 patients over 164 square km (450 square miles). She was the first ever Native American doctor and she was a woman—she broke down huge barriers for her gender and for the Native American people. Her tireless devotion to the welfare of her community—teaching people how to protect their health and their civil rights—changed their lives, but many believe her story remains largely untold and that there is still work to be done in giving her due credit and remembrance for all she achieved.

In 2009, a modern resident of the Omaha Reservation said: "We need streets named after her. We need her life to be taught in schools. We need her attitude toward education and helping people to permeate throughout this reservation. She could be a role model to our young people, but no one knows … her story."

In 2014 Dennis Hastings, Omaha Reservation member and historian, wrote: "Dr. Susan could very well emerge as one of the more notable heroines in American history."

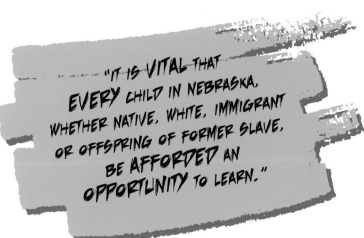

"IT IS VITAL THAT EVERY CHILD IN NEBRASKA, WHETHER NATIVE, WHITE, IMMIGRANT OR OFFSPRING OF FORMER SLAVE, BE AFFORDED AN OPPORTUNITY TO LEARN."

RUBBING ALCOHOL COMPOUND

MARIE THARP

SNAKES AND MUD PIES

Marie Tharp was a twentieth-century geologist, whose work mapping the North Atlantic Ocean Floor led to a vastly improved understanding of the evolution of Earth's crust.

Marie Tharp was born on July 30, 1920, in Ypsilanti, Michigan, USA, to William Edgar Tharp and Bertha Louise Newton, who were respectively 50 and 40 years old at the time. Marie's father had worked in a plant (gardening) nursery until the US Department of Agriculture's Bureau of Soils hired him to work for them as a soil expert in 1904. Marie's mother Bertha taught German in high-school, though she died at the age of 55, when Marie was 15 years old. As the only child of older parents, Marie was doted on by William and Bertha, but at the same time

"I GUESS I HAD MAP-MAKING IN MY BLOOD, THOUGH I HADN'T PLANNED TO FOLLOW IN MY FATHER'S FOOTSTEPS."

they encouraged her to be an independent thinker, particularly when it came to her education. They wanted Marie to explore as much as possible before she decided what she wanted for her future. For most of her childhood, her father's job meant that the family moved regularly—every season—following the changes in "soft" soil. They spent summers in the north and winters in the south of the country, and every four years they moved to Washington DC, to the Bureau of Soils' main office, so that William could oversee printing of the soil maps he'd worked on in the years in between.

For much of her early life, Marie showed no particular interest in science, but she loved spending time with her father in the soil fields. She would sit in the back of his truck, making mud pies, and also trekked with him into the countryside. Spending so much time outdoors, examining the wonders of nature with her father, must have had an impact on the young Marie, forging a connection with the natural world that would blossom in later life. She attended more than a dozen schools, and before graduating from high school she spent a year in Florence, Alabama, where she went on regular field trips to study trees and rocks—once finding and collecting a bag of snake skeletons and skins that horrified her mother when Marie brought them home to show her. It was during this time in Florence, Alabama, that Marie took a class called Current Science. Here, she learned of the latest work and advances in different scientific fields. However, it was not until she graduated from high school that the study of science really appealed to her, or that her future career took shape in her mind.

THE PG GIRL

In 1939, Marie entered Ohio University, starting out studying Art as a main subject, then Music, German, Zoology, Paleobotany, Philosophy, and English—before meeting a professor called Dr. Dow, who was to become her mentor and helped forge her love of Geology. Dr. Dow recognized Marie's flair and passion for geological science, and also encouraged her to take up drafting, which is making technical drawings—a discipline that would increase Marie's chances of getting a job in a world still dominated by men. Drafting gave her useful skills, and trained her to see the geological world from many different dimensions.

At the beginning of World War II, when Marie was a senior student at college, she spotted a note on the college bulletin board that offered an "accelerated"—or quick—geology degree, with the promise of a job in the petroleum industry on graduation. Since many men had been called up into the military services to fight in the war, women had greater career opportunities, and the year after she graduated from Ohio with a degree in Music and English, Marie began a two-year

degree in Petroleum Geology at the University of Michigan. Here, she was one of a group of women known as the "PG Girls."

At the time, there was still no definite theory on how Earth's crust had formed, and not enough was known about the formation of mountains, oceans, continents, and islands. Experts could not agree— even a leading text book on the subject at the time said that this area of science was still a mystery. A visiting geologist to Michigan told her team that a geologist's best tool is to be able to see an incomplete picture of the natural world and make an "educated guess" as to its origins. This inspired Marie to work hard to make the best-possible educated guesses in geology that she could.

In addition to her coursework, Marie spent the rest of her degree at Michigan, taking as many extra classes as possible in Mathematics, Physics, and Chemistry. It was this intense and varied studying that helped her to make informed geological calculations in her future career, and laid the foundations for her first important field discovery.

"I WAS SO BUSY MAKING MAPS I LET THEM ARGUE."

MAPPING THE OCEAN FLOOR

After leaving Michigan with a master's degree in Geology, Marie got an office job working for Standard Oil in Tulsa, Oklahoma, during which time she studied for and earned another degree in Mathematics. Following that, in 1948, she moved to New York to work for the highly regarded geologist Maurice Ewing in the Lamont Geological Observatory at Columbia University, initially as a research assistant. Spotting her ambition and skill, as well as her dislike of office work, Ewing later invited her to become part of the team in his newly formed geophysical laboratory at Columbia, and she jumped at the chance. In 1952, she was assigned to work with the geologist Bruce Heezen, and they began what was to be a 25-year partnership—their first assignment was to locate aircraft from World War II that had crashed into the sea. They then moved on to analyzing sound recordings of the ocean floor to discover more about how it was formed. At the time, women were not permitted to go on most ships, so while Bruce worked at sea, Marie used her drafting skills to create maps

that made sense of the sonar readings that Bruce sent back to her. Her work with Bruce was the first systematic attempt to map the entire ocean floor.

Marie made a number of "profiles" of the North Atlantic Ocean—stretching from Martha's Vineyard on the northeastern coast of the USA to Recife in Brazil. Using temperature readings, salt measurements, and core—or rock—measurements, she discovered a rock valley—or rift—stretching down the middle of the Mid-Atlantic Ridge of the ocean. Marie's important theory on how this valley had formed went against the beliefs of the time, and was first dismissed by many, including Bruce, who called it "girl talk." It was through the work of another scientist, hired by Bruce to examine earthquakes, that Marie's "educated guess" about the rift valley was proved absolutely right.

By now often able to work at sea for limited periods, Marie continued her work on extending the map of the North Atlantic rift valley, finding similar rift structures in other oceans around the world. Then she made her most thrilling discovery— a 65,000-km (40,000-mile) oceanic rift valley. By 1977, Marie and Bruce published their groundbreaking map of the entire ocean floor: World Ocean Floor Panorama—a map that is used widely in geological departments and text books today.

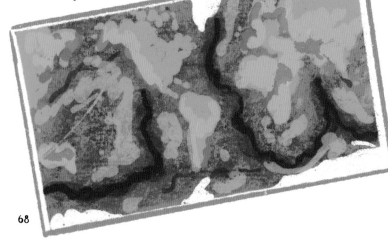

PIONEER OF OCEANOGRAPHY

Marie Tharp died of cancer on August 23, 2006, at the age of 86, having excelled at the "educated guesses" she made about the structure and formation of our Earth. After Bruce Heezen's death, she continued to work at Columbia University until 1983, when she was 63. After she left Columbia, though she was supposed to be enjoying her retirement, she set up and operated a map-distribution business. Then later, in 1995, she donated her precious map collection and the notes she'd made to the Map and Geography Division of the Library of Congress in the US.

Today, the Mid-Atlantic Ridge that Marie mapped is viewed as vital evidence for seafloor spreading and continental drift—where magma boils up from inside Earth's mantle and through the crust and is cooled and pushed away. But at the time of her work, her observations—and the complete map of the ocean floor that resulted from her collaboration with Heezen—were dismissed. The reaction to her work was compared later to the relevation of first seeing photographs of Earth from space—it had to be seen to be believed.

"There's truth to the old cliché that a picture is worth a thousand words and that seeing is believing," Marie once wrote. We can't see what lies at the bottom of the sea, or farther beneath Earth's crust, but thanks to Marie's careful calculations we know now what it looks like and our understanding of our planet's landscape has been transformed.

Marie did come to receive full recognition for her great contribution to geological science. In 1997, she was named as one of the four greatest cartographers of the twentieth century by the Library of Congress, which included her work in an exhibit in the 100th-anniversary celebration of its Geography and Map Division. Then in 2001, she was given the first annual Lamont-Doherty Earth Observatory Heritage Award for her life's work as a pioneer of oceanography. In 2009, Google Earth added the Marie Tharp Historical Map layer, so that people could view her ocean map using the Google Earth interface. And in 2015, the International Astronomical Union named a moon crater after her.

"INTELLIGENCE IS THE ABILITY TO ADAPT TO CHANGE."

STEPHEN HAWKING

THE YOUNG INVENTOR

Stephen Hawking is regarded as one of the most brilliant theoretical physicists in history, whose work on the origins of the Universe—from the Big Bang theory to black holes to string theory—revolutionized the scientific field of cosmology. Born on January 8, 1942, in Oxford, England to Frank and Isobel Hawking, Stephen had two younger sisters and an adopted younger brother. Though both of his parents came from families who had financial difficulties, each had attended Oxford University—his father had studied medicine and his mother had studied Philosophy, Politics, and Economics.

Stephen struggled to learn to read at his first school in Highgate, London. When Stephen was 8 years old, his father started working at the National Institute for Medical Research and the family moved to the town of St. Albans in Hertfordshire, where they were considered both highly intelligent and quite eccentric. Their house was large, untidy, and crammed with books and furniture—and the family car was a converted London cab. Frank and Isobel Hawking placed a high value on education. On

arrival in Hertfordshire, Stephen briefly went to St. Albans High School for Girls—where younger boys were allowed to attend. In 1952—having passed the entrance exam a year early at the age of 10—he started at St. Albans School. Here, Stephen formed a close group of friends. Together they played board games; made fireworks, model planes, and boats; and had long discussions about religion. They even built a computer, recycling among other things clock parts and an old telephone switchboard.

Though Stephen was clearly intelligent, and was known at school as "Einstein," his gift for science was not obvious until he was in his teens, when he decided he wanted to study mathematics at university. In fact, his father advised him to study medicine instead, as he thought there would be better job prospects after graduation. Frank wanted his son to go to University College, Oxford, as he had, but because at that time there was no course in mathematics at the college, Stephen went for his second choice of study, physics and chemistry.

LIFE-CHANGING NEWS

In 1959, at the age of 17, Hawking was awarded a scholarship to Oxford University. In his first year there, he was lonely and bored—and he found the coursework too easy. It was only in his second and third years, when he made more effort to fit in, that he became outgoing and popular and decided to join the college rowing club. His rowing coach later said that Stephen had a reputation as a daredevil—encouraging the rest of his crew to take risky routes that often led to mishaps and damaged boats.

Hawking once worked out that he'd studied for only about 1,000 hours during his three years at Oxford. These poor study habits meant that he didn't do well in his final exams. He hoped to go on to do graduate study at Cambridge University, for which he needed a first-class degree, and his results from Oxford were just on the border between a first- and second-class degree. This meant he had to pass an oral exam in order to get into Cambridge. He knew that his tutors thought he was lazy and difficult, but he was also confident that they would see his potential. He was right. Despite his attitude, his examiners realized they had a very gifted student on their hands and granted him a first-class degree in physics. In October 1962, after taking a trip to Iran with a friend, he began his graduate work at Trinity Hall, Cambridge.

It was during his second year at Cambridge, when he was 21, that Hawking was diagnosed with Motor Neurone Disease—a condition which progressively damages the nerves and causes muscles to waste away—and he fell into a depression. Doctors advised him to carry on with his graduate studies, but at first he didn't see the point. Even though his condition advanced more slowly than predicted, he soon had difficulty walking and speaking, and was given just two years to live—though that diagnosis turned out to be wildly inaccurate. It was grim news, but with his tutor's encouragement, Stephen began focusing on his studies again—and even with his physical challenges, his reputation for brilliance grew.

When he'd begun his degree at Cambridge, theories around the creation of the Universe and the Big Bang were hotly debated, but Stephen was sure he had something new and important to contribute to this debate. He developed his own theory, inspired by cosmologist Roger Penrose's theory of "space-time singularity," and then wrote a paper laying out his calculations. His thesis was approved and won him a research post at another college in Cambridge to study applied mathematics and theoretical physics, specializing in general relativity and cosmology. By March 1966, Hawking had not only defied the odds with his disease and earned his Ph.D., but he had also made the first of many groundbreaking advances into our understanding of the Universe. And though his disease now meant he needed a wheelchair to get around, he had found personal happiness with his first wife, Jane Wilde—whom he'd married in 1965, a year before graduating from Cambridge.

"I'M NOT AFRAID OF DEATH, BUT I'M IN NO HURRY TO DIE. I HAVE SO MUCH I WANT TO DO FIRST."
BLACK HOLE
SINGULARITY

THE BIG BANG AND BLACK HOLES

Stephen Hawking worked at Cambridge after his graduation, as a researcher and professor, and began a lifetime's career studying the basic laws governing the Universe. Among other things, he worked out that just as the Universe, while infinite, has a beginning—the Big Bang—it must also have an ending, and one day it will disappear.

In 1966, he began working with Roger Penrose, whose theories had inspired him to produce his own first great theory. And in 1970, together they suggested what became known as the "second law of black hole dynamics"—that the surface of a black hole can never get smaller. Hawking also showed that Einstein's theory of general relativity strongly hints that space and time began with the Big Bang and ends within "black holes"—objects in space that are so dense and have such a strong gravitational pull that not even light can escape from their grasp. Penrose and Hawking's demonstration meant that Einstein's theory and quantum theory (the existence of the smallest possible matter) are connected. Blending these two theories, Stephen also revealed that black holes are not completely black—or dark—but that they give out radiation—a theory that was later known as "Hawking radiation."

In 1974, Hawking was invited to become a Fellow of the Royal Society, a global team of elite scientists, and in the same year he left Britain to spend a year working at a university in California, returning to Cambridge in 1975, to a more senior post in gravitational physics. It was a time when both scientists and society in general were becoming fascinated by black holes, and as a leading expert in the subject, Hawking was regularly interviewed for newspapers and on television.

In 1979, Stephen was appointed to the prestigious role of Lucasian Professor at Cambridge University, though by that time his frail health meant that he needed nurses to help care for him at home. He continued to study hard over the years, digging deeper into his subject—even importantly challenging some of his earlier theories on black holes. In 2014, he controversially claimed that "there are no black holes"—at least not in the way that cosmologist understood them. He proposed a radical new understanding of these phenomena, and also argued that the Universe has no boundaries and it is possible to travel around and through it into infinity.

In his first book on the subject of black holes and the Universe, *A Brief History of Time*, Hawking aimed to ask and answer questions about the birth and death of the Universe for non-scientific minds. This book was published in 1988, and was so successful that it remains an international bestseller today.

"MY *DISABILITIES* HAVE NOT BEEN A SIGNIFICANT HANDICAP IN MY FIELD, WHICH IS THEORETICAL PHYSICS. INDEED, THEY HAVE HELPED ME IN A WAY BY *SHIELDING ME* FROM LECTURING AND ADMINISTRATIVE WORK THAT I WOULD OTHERWISE HAVE BEEN INVOLVED IN."

LEGACY

Stephen Hawking died in Cambridge on March 14, 2018, at the age of 76. Fittingly, he was born on the 300th university of Galileo's death—and died on the 139th anniversary of Albert Einstein's birth. Such was his enormous influence—despite his debilitating disease—that tributes came not just from scientists, but from people of all backgrounds and throughout the world. At Gonville and Caius College in Cambridge, a flag was flown at half mast in recognition of his status in the science community and many high-profile people at his funeral.

Hawking's scientific work has inspired generations of students to study problems of gravity and quantum mechanics. Since his death many of his colleagues have written of his huge scientific accomplishments—in particular, his work on "classical gravity" and "singularities," his famous results on black-hole thermodynamics and Hawking radiation, and his efforts to quantize gravity. Professor Chris Imafidon, who consulted Hawking in 2007 about encouraging higher level mathematics students, said: "He is not just a scientist; he is an inspiration … He sees 100 years into the future."

Toward the end of his life, Stephen could not speak without the aid of a machine, or move his hands or legs, but in spite of this he never stopped questioning and talking about the universe beyond Earth—mentally, he was exploring a realm that is bigger and more mysterious than we might ever know. His ambition to the end was to connect our understanding of infinitely small particles and atoms with the infinitely large scale of the cosmos through his "string theory"—strings being tiny tubes of energy.

Hawking became a cultural icon on TV, appearing regularly as himself on TV's *The Big Bang Theory* and as a cartoon in *The Simpsons*. More seriously, he gave his final television interview—on the detection of gravitational waves caused by the collision of two neutron stars—in October 2017. A year later, another of his final research studies, entitled "Black Hole Entropy and Soft Hair"—which looked into the mystery of what happens to the information held by objects once they disappear into a black hole—was published. And his final book, *Brief Answers to the Big Questions*, aimed once more to give all of us some insight into an incredibly complex subject.

Stephen Hawking's unique and brilliant mind was matched by determination and resourcefulness in the face of great physical and mental challenges, which arguably focused his mind all the better on his subject. His relentless quest to know more and to know better is a message to humankind to never stop asking questions when it comes to the future of our Earth, the planets that surround it, and, of course, the Universe that encircles it all.

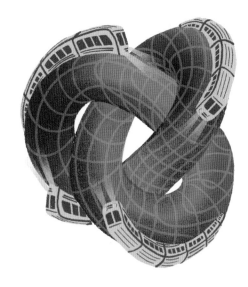

A **STUD**IOUS **CHILD**

Chien-Shiung Wu was a Chinese American physicist, who was also known as the "Queen of Nuclear Research" due to her considerable contribution to the world of nuclear physics. She is most famous for her work on the "Wu Experiment," but was also a vital part of the Manhattan Project, which tested for and assembled the first atomic bomb during World War II.

Chien-Shiung Wu was born on May 31, 1912, in the town of Liuhe in Taicang, in Jiangsu province, China. She was the only daughter and middle sibling of three children born to Wu Zhong-Yi and his wife Fan Fu-Hua. Her father had been an engineer before he participated in the 1911 revolution that ended Manchu rule by the Qing dynasty in China, and her mother was a teacher. As part of the family tradition, all children had "Chien" as the first of their names—Chien-Shiung Wu's older brother was Chien-Ying and her younger brother was Chien-Hao.

Education was very important to Chien-Shiung Wu's parents. Her father, with whom she was very close, encouraged her to pursue science and mathematics and was passionate that she had a childhood spent learning and exploring as much

as possible. He filled their home with books and newspapers to broaden Chien-Shiung Wu's education from an early age. Her formal primary education was at Ming De School—set up by her father and one of the first schools in China to admit girls. Then, at the age of 9, Chien-Shiung Wu left Liuhe to go to the Suzhou Women's Normal School—a boarding school that incorporated teacher training along with regular tuition for its students. The course was highly competitive and based on merit, though some families paid for their child's place.

Chien-Shiung Wu's family could have afforded to pay, but she chose to work hard and earn her way on to the course through study instead. This approach paid off, as Chien-Shiung Wu's grades earned her 9th place of 10,000 applicants. She graduated from the Sozhou school in 1930, at the top of her class, and was accepted for admission to the National Central University in Nanjing. By state law, before she could begin studying to be a teacher at the university, she had to work for a year in a school, so Chien-Shiung Wu taught at a public school in Shanghai run by the philosopher Hu Shih.

FROM CHINA TO THE USA

Chien-Shiung Wu started her course at the National Central University in 1930—first to study mathematics, then physics—and while she was there she became active in politics. At the time, Japan was threatening to invade China, and Chien-Shung Wu quickly got involved in the university protests—leading the student plea that China take a stronger political stance against the Japanese. She was a top student, consistently scoring high marks, so even though she led a sit-in at the Presidential Palace in Nanjing it did not damage her academic prospects.

Chien-Shiung Wu graduated from National Central University in 1934, and spent the next two years studying physics at graduate level, working as an assistant and also as a researcher at the Institute of Physics at Zheijang University. Here, she was encouraged to apply to the University of Michigan in the USA to do her Ph.D., and with financial help from her uncle she was awarded a place. In 1936, accompanied by a student friend, Chien-Shiung Wu then set sail for the west coast

of the US on the SS *President Hoover*. As her family waved her off, she had no idea she would never see them again.

Chien-Shiung Wu's plans changed soon after she arrived in San Francisco when she visited a physicist called Luke Chia-Liu Yuan at the University of California, Berkeley. Berkeley's impressive radiation laboratory, and its director Ernest O. Lawrence—a rising star in science who was later awarded the Nobel Prize for Physics—greatly appealed to Chien-Shiung Wu. Having heard that at the University of Michigan women were viewed as second-class citizens, she made up her mind to give up her place at Michigan and study at Berkeley instead. She was denied a place on the university course, but luckily she was offered a place to study in the radiation laboratory instead.

At the Berkeley laboratory, Chien-Shiung Wu made impressive progress working toward her thesis, which was in two parts. One part was on electromagnetic radiation, including "beta decay," on which she would later become an expert. The other part was on the production of radioactive isotopes, and nuclear fission of uranium, for which she experimented in the university radiation laboratory. Four years later, in 1940, Chien-Shiung Wu completed her Ph.D., and stayed on to work at the Radiation Laboratory as a researcher.

"...THERE IS ONLY ONE THING WORSE THAN COMING HOME FROM THE LAB TO A SINK FULL OF DIRTY DISHES, AND THAT IS NOT GOING TO THE LAB AT ALL!"

FIRST LADY OF PRINCETON

"BETA DECAY WAS ... LIKE A DEAR OLD FRIEND. THERE WOULD ALWAYS BE A SPECIAL PLACE IN MY HEART RESERVED ESPECIALLY FOR IT."

In 1942, a couple of years after the start of World War II, Chien-Shiung Wu married Luke Chia-Liu Yuan—though none of their parents could attend the wedding due to the outbreak of the Pacific War. The couple moved to the east coast of America, where Chien-Shiung Wu began work at Smith College—a private women's college in Massachusetts. She found this job frustrating, as her duties only involved teaching and there was little opportunity for research, but her talent and hard work meant she was later promoted to an associate professor at the college, and also given a pay rise. After a few years, Chien-Shiung Wu accepted an offer from Princeton University to be the first female instructor ever to work there.

In 1944, Chien-Shiung Wu became part of the Manhattan Project at Columbia University, where she discovered a way to improve the quality of uranium ore as fuel for an atomic bomb. After the end of the war in August 1945, Chien-Shiung Wu became a US citizen and had a son with Yuan. She left the Manhattan Project and began work at the Department of Physics at Columbia. Over the years, she became the leading experimentalist in beta decay and "weak interaction physics." It was in 1956, however, that she had her greatest achievement, the Wu Experiment, which was conducted at a laboratory in Washington. Chien-Shiung Wu led a team that included male physicists Tsung-Dao Lee and Chen-Ning Yang, who used "cobalt-60" —a radioactive form of cobalt metal— to successfully challenge a previously

firmly held theory about a law of physics, known as the law of parity. This discovery was a major breakthrough in physics, but as a woman Chien-Shiung Wu was denied the Nobel Prize for her vital work on it. Instead the prize was given to Chen Ning Yang and Tsung-Dao Lee. Chien-Shiung Wu said later: "I wonder whether the tiny atoms and nuclei, or the mathematical symbols, or the DNA molecules have any preference for either masculine or feminine treatment."

Chien-Shiung Wu was made a full Professor at Columbia University in 1958—the first woman to hold this position in the physics department there. For the rest of her career, she researched the biophysics of sickle-cell disease—a life-shortening condition that attacks the immune system. In 1981, she retired from Columbia University and devoted herself to promoting women's work in STEM (Science, Technology, Engineering, and Mathematics), becoming a role model for young female scientists everywhere.

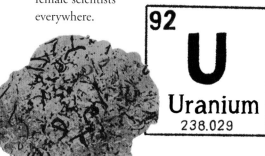

92
U
Uranium
238.029

MENTOR OF MANY

Chien-Shiung Wu died at the age of 84, on February 16, 1997, in New York City and was cremated. Her ashes were buried in the grounds of her old school in China, and in 2002, a bronze statue of her was placed in the courtyard of Ming De School to commemorate her.

Chien-Shung Wu's revelation about the theory of parity was a revolutionary step in the field of nuclear physics, and all the more important because it reinforced the fact that women could make influential contributions to science, particularly in the field of nuclear physics, a field then dominated by men. By the 1950s, the "conservation of physical properties" was a key idea idea in physics. It had been demonstrated that important physical properties of particles, such as mass, energy, momentum, and electrical charge, are the same before and after a nuclear reaction. Chien-Shiung Wu's theory caused physicists to rethink some basic assumptions and was also valuable in explaining some otherwise puzzling experimental results in nuclear physics. Her work stimulated research in the progressive investigation of "symmetry"—conducted by influential physicists, including Richard Feynman, Murray Gell-Mann, Robert Marshak, Ennackel Chandy, and George Sudarshan.

In her lifetime Chien-Shiung Wu was given many accolades, including in 1958 being made the first woman to earn the Research Corporation Award, and she was the seventh woman to be elected to the National Academy of Sciences. In 1962, she received the John Price Wetherill Medal of the Franklin Institute and was awarded the

"A GLIMPSE OF THIS WONDER CAN BE THE REWARD OF A LIFETIME. COULD IT BE THAT EXCITEMENT AND ENNOBLING FEELINGS LIKE THESE HAVE KEPT US SCIENTISTS MARCHING FORWARD FOREVER?"

National Medal of Science in 1975. In 1990, the Chinese Academy of Sciences named asteroid 2752 Wu Chien-Shiung after her, and in 1995, the Wu Chien-Shiung Education Foundation was founded to provide scholarships to young scientists. In 1998, a year after her death, Wu was admitted into the American National Women's Hall of Fame. In a life dedicated to science, Chien-Shiung Wu mentored dozens of aspiring scientists, including her son, Vincent Yuan, who became a physicist himself. She was a trailblazer, breaking down barriers not just for the science community in general, but for all women in the workplace.

ABRAHAM NEMETH

FEELING LETTERS

Abraham was born in Manhattan, New York, on October 16, 1918, into a family of Hungarian Jews. He was blind from birth, and at the time of his childhood, visually impaired children were not expected to achieve or contribute much to society; instead they were taught menial or manual work, such as weaving baskets and stitching pillowcases. But Abraham Nemeth's Jewish immigrant parents did not accept these low social expectations for their son. Instead, his father would regularly walk with Abraham around the local streets, encouraging him to touch raised lettering on mailboxes and fire hydrants so that he would learn the shapes of printed letters, and come to have a sense of direction. As Manhattan's layout was and is based on a grid, this routine was vital to his growing independence. Abraham's mother would often send him as a 6-year-old to his grandfather's grocery store around the corner to pick up things like bread, butter, and sour cream. Both his parents were keen to prepare him for his bar mitzvah—the Jewish coming-of-age ritual for boys—and to teach him that there was nothing he couldn't do, despite his disability.

Abraham was educated at the New York Guild for the Jewish Blind in Yonkers—an inner suburb of New York City. At the time there was no Braille enabling him to read Hebrew, so he learned Biblical and Jewish traditions by sitting with his grandfather and listening to him read aloud. It was as a teenager that Abraham developed a passion for mathematics, but when he began studying at Brooklyn College he was encouraged to study psychology instead because learning complex mathematics without being able to see was considered almost impossible.

"IT IS TRUE THAT I AM BLIND, BUT I AM NOT THE ONE WHO IS LOST."

BIG BREAK

After he left Brooklyn College in 1940, Abraham found it very difficult to find a job as a psychologist, and was told his prospects would improve if he studied for a master's degree in the subject. He then applied for and was accepted on a course in psychology at Columbia University in New York—where he earned his Ph.D. degree in 1942.

Even with his Ph.D., work in his chosen field was hard to come by for Abraham. He was a self-taught musician and on graduation from Columbia he earned money by playing the piano in clubs around Brooklyn, meeting his soon-to-be first wife, Florence Weismann, in the early 1940s. After they got married in 1944, Abraham took a job at the American Foundation for the Blind, where he stitched pillow cases, loaded boxes of talking-book records onto trucks, and counted phonograph needles into envelopes. He was nowhere near the career in psychology that had been decided for him, but his attraction for mathematics was stronger than ever. In his spare time, he took mathematics courses at both Brooklyn College and Columbia University. For him, learning how to do complex calculations and equations was as relaxing as going bowling might be for anyone else. It was a passionate hobby, and something he still wanted to take up as a career.

It was in 1945, when Abraham volunteered to tutor returning World War II soldiers in calculus, that his first big break came. As he chalked equations up on the board, explaining the process to his soldier students, he didn't know that he was being observed by another professor. He then received the telegram that altered the course of his professional life. One of the teachers in the mathematics department had become ill, and Abraham was asked to fill in for him until he recovered.

Following this stint as a supply teacher, Abraham was inspired to go back to Columbia University and work on a Ph.D. degree in mathematics. Florence encouraged him in this—even if jobs in the field might be hard to come by for a blind man. "Wouldn't you rather be an unemployed mathematician than an unemployed psychologist?" she told him. Abraham didn't hesitate—he resigned fully from his job at the American Foundation for the Blind and started studying for a degree in mathematics.

"MATHEMATICIANS ARE INTRINSICALLY LAZY CREATURES. THEY SPEND YEARS TRYING TO FIND AN EASIER WAY TO DO THINGS."

THE NEMETH CODE

Early in his pursuit of sophisticated mathematics, and frustrated that there was no Braille code designed for calculations beyond basic arithmetic, Abraham had begun developing a private code to support complicated calculations. While he'd been working at the American Foundation for the Blind, he became friendly with a man called Clifford Witcher, who came to him later, eager to be able to read complex mathematical sums, too. Abraham wasn't sure that the code he'd invented for himself would work for his friend, but agreed to teach it to him anyway. Clifford Witcher happened to be a member of the Joint Uniform Braille Committee—the equivalent in the 1950s of what is now the Braille Authority of North America. Abraham's self-designed Braille impressed Clifford so much that he relayed it to his colleagues on the committee, who then asked Abraham to prepare them a report on his code. Abraham delivered his report to the JUBC one morning in 1951, and by the afternoon the Nemeth Code was named and adopted as an official mathematical code for the blind.

Meanwhile, Abraham continued to push himself hard, driven by the self-reliance he'd been taught by his parents. He accepted every job he was offered, whether it was part-time teaching or a one-night piano gig in a bar. He still routinely went on trains and buses, as well as walking, throughout Manhattan and Brooklyn, to maintain his skills in orientation—and he did all of this without the use of a white cane. Certainly, in the 1930s and 1940s, the white sticks that the visually impaired have now were not in regular use. Abraham and others like him were forced to rely on what resources they had—patience, common sense, and routine. It wasn't until 1955 that Abraham began using a white cane—the same year that he moved with Florence to Michigan, where he'd landed a full-time teaching post at the University of Detroit.

Abraham spent the next 30 years teaching graduate and undergraduate mathematics courses at the University of Detroit. While there, he completed his post-graduate work at Wayne State University and earned his Ph.D. in mathematics. During the 1960s he founded the computer science department at the University of Detroit and he continued to teach that subject, as well as mathematics, until his retirement in 1985.

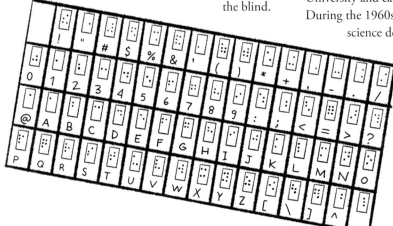

CHANGING LIVES

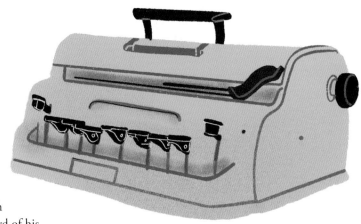

Abraham Nemeth died on October 2, 2013, at the age of 95. Up until his death it was said he was as sharp as a man a third of his age, and beloved for his intelligence, wit, musical ability, and charisma—along with his optimism and love of life. He achieved a huge amount in spite and because of his lifelong blindness, improving the lives and prospects of the visually impaired all over the world for generations to come.

After retiring, and leaving Detroit University in 1985, Abraham did not stop working. He became an active member of the National Federation of the Blind, attending its national convention every year until 2011. And he continued his work on a standardized form of Braille, the Nemeth Uniform Braille System—or NUBS—which combined existing forms of Braille for mathematics, literature, and computer use. This work has transformed the lives and prospects of blind mathematicians the world over.

In later life, Abraham was also a fierce advocate for the blind in Michigan, and he fought to have a Braille bill passed in that state so that future generations of blind children would have the opportunity to learn Braille. He continued his work with the Jewish Braille Institute International to revise Jewish prayer books, in English and Hebrew, so that any visually impaired person going to the synagogue—Jewish temple—would need just a single prayer book to take part in any religious service. This changed the lives of the blind Jewish community. In 2006 he finished composing the English Braille for a Hebrew-English version of a best-selling *siddur*—or prayer book. The same year, he received the Louis Braille Award in recognition of his lifetime's work.

In Abraham Nemeth's obituary for the National Federation of the Blind, he is fondly recalled in his apartment—surrounded by his Braille books in all subjects, and his numerous awards, including a bust of Louis Braille—quoting his grandfather in relation to how he has dealt with the challenges of being a blind man: "It is better to light a candle," said Abraham, "than to curse the dark."

"EXPECT FROM A BLIND CHILD WHAT YOU EXPECT FROM A SIGHTED CHILD."

VALENTINA TERESHKOVA

PARACHUTES AND SPACESHIPS

Valentina Tereshkova—also known as "Valya"—was born on March 6, 1937, in Bolshoye Maslennikovo, which is a village on the Volga River in western Russia. She was the second of Vladimir and Elena Tereshkova's three children. Her father Vladimir was a tractor driver, who served as a Russian army soldier during World War II, until Valentina was two years old, when he was killed in action. Valentina's mother Elena then raised her as well as her sister Ludmilla and her brother, also called Vladimir, by herself, working in a local textile mill to support the family financially.

Young Valentina helped her mother around the house from an early age, and so only began going to school when she was around 9 years old. In 1954, at the age of 17, she moved to live with her grandmother in nearby Yaroslavl, where she worked as an apprentice in a factory. In 1955, she joined her mother and sister Ludmilla in the cotton mill, where she was a loom operator. She did, however, continue her education through a correspondence course, and graduated from the Light Industry

Technical School. At this time, Valentina believed in communist values—that society should be equal and without a class system, and that people should not own personal property. She became a member of the cotton mill's "Komsomol," or Young Communist League, before becoming a full member of the Communist Party.

In 1959, at the age of 22, Valentina joined the Yaroslavl Air Sports Club and developed a strong passion for parachuting. She worked hard at her hobby, and by the early 1960s had become a skilled amateur parachutist. This was about the time that the first expeditions into space were happening, and Valentina was fascinated by space travel. Her hero was Yuri Gagarin, the Soviet cosmonaut who in 1961 became the first person to travel into space on board the spacecraft *Vostok 1*. Valentina was determined to one day become a cosmonaut, too.

TRAILBLAZER

"ONCE YOU'VE BEEN IN SPACE, YOU REALIZE HOW SMALL AND FRAGILE THE EARTH IS."

During the late 1950s and 1960s, the Space Race between the United States and the Soviet Union was highly competitive. Both countries were determined to achieve space travel "supremacy"—and be the best in that field. It was the Soviets who were determined to send the first woman into space, however. Because being able to parachute from a capsule in Earth's atmosphere is a vital part of a cosmonaut's role, the Soviet Space Agency put word out that they were looking for skilled parachutists to train as candidates for space flight. Valentina jumped at the opportunity. She had no experience as a pilot, but she had made an impressive 126 parachute jumps, so she put herself forward for selection.

Competition to become the first female space pilot was fierce, but in the end four candidates were chosen to compete with each other for a one-time-only space flight. Valentina Tereshkova was one of them. Like the other three women, she underwent a difficult training course for 18 months. This included being tested to see how she could deal with being alone for long periods of time, along with how well she coped with extreme gravity conditions and weightlessness. Valentina, who proved resilient in all these areas, outshone her competitors and was finally selected to be the first woman space pilot, at which point she was given a rank in the Soviet Air Force.

In June 1963, Valentina climbed into the spacecraft, *Vostok 6*, and made history, as well as the most exciting journey of her life. She flew up into space, orbiting—or circling—Earth 48 times in just under 3 days. This was a world record—even her hero Yuri Gagarin had only orbited Earth once, and the 4 American astronauts who had flown before Valentina orbited it a total of 36 times. The nation was thrilled for her success, and the Soviet president told her: "Valentina, I am very happy and proud that a girl from the Soviet Union is the first woman to fly into space and to operate such cutting-edge equipment."

Valentina Tereshkova returned from her voyage—parachuting down from her spacecraft to Earth from 6,000 m (20,000 ft)—and was promptly awarded the title of "Hero of the Soviet Union."

LEGACY

It was 19 years after Valentina Tereshkova's groundbreaking flight before another woman went into space—another Russian named Svetlana Savitskaya. In America, the first woman to travel into space was Sally Ride, more than two decades after Valentina, in 1983. It has been reported that female astronauts were not treated equally to their male counterparts, which might explain their long absence from space travel.

In the years following her flight, Valentina remained in the military and graduated with top marks from the Zhukovosky Military Air Academy in 1969. After this, as well as becoming a leading member of the Communist Party, she was a representative for the USSR—Union of Soviet Socialist Republics—at many international events, including at the United Nations conference for the International Women's Year in 1975. Between 1968 and 1987, she also led the Committee of Soviet Women.

She is still active in the space community, and her legacy as the first ever female astronaut is recognized and celebrated throughout the world, in books, in museums, and as the subject of stage plays. In 2017, the Science Museum in London ran a temporary exhibition named "Valentina Tereshkova: First Woman in Space," which consisted of photographs and various objects of historic interest from her life. In the same year, the stage director Valentina Fratti—who was herself named after Tereshkova—produced a play off Broadway in New York City entitled *They Promised Her the Moon*. Partly a tribute to Valentina Tereshkova, the play was also about the early life of Jerrie Cobb, an American pilot who tried, but unlike Valentina, failed to fly into space. Shortly after this, another play entitled *Moonshot* included Valentina as one of its central characters.

The impact of her mission, even decades after she made it, was such that she was a central part of a 2014 BBC documentary: *Cosmonauts: How Russia Won the Space Race*, which was seen from the Soviet perspective through examination of certain documents that had been kept secret by the government until then.

Valentina's love of space travel has not faded over the years. When *Vostok 6* was exhibited at the Science Museum in London, she talked about it as one of the loves of her life, describing it as "my best and most beautiful friend." She has also said that if she could afford it she would love to fly to Mars.

From such humble beginnings, Valentina Tereshkova is a real-life action hero, who has twice carried the Olympic Torch for her country. Her resourcefulness and determination overcame the odds against any woman pursuing the traditionally male role of cosmonaut. She has been an inspiration for all women who have walked in her footsteps, and a testament to the power of dreaming big.

JOHN FORBES NASH JR.

SOLITARY CHILD

Throughout his life, John Forbes Nash Jr. experienced a form of schizophrenia that drove people away. And yet his contribution to the field of game theory has transformed international diplomacy and may even have helped to prevent wars.

John Forbes Nash Jr. was born on June 13, 1928, in Bluefield, West Virginia. His father, John Forbes Nash Sr., was an electrical engineer, and his mother, Margaret Virginia Nash, had been a schoolteacher up until she got married. John's sister Martha was two years younger than him. John—or Johnny, as he was known—was raised in a close, loving family. A keen reader, he was a quiet, introverted boy, preferring to play on his own with toy planes and cars than to join in with other children's games. His mother encouraged his clear interest in reading and science. She made sure he had good schooling, and even taught him at home. His father is said to have treated him like an adult, giving him dense science books to read rather than children's books.

At first, John did not reveal a particular ability for any subject at school—his schoolteachers referred to him as "backward." With hindsight it is likely that he was bored, finding the school work too easy— something that was also said of Stephen Hawking and Albert Einstein in their early schooling. By the age of 12, John was more interested in carrying out experiments in his bedroom at home than he was in the classroom. Though his parents continued to encourage him to be more sociable, he disliked sport and organized dances, and remained a loner. His sister Martha said much later that "Johnny was always different … He always wanted to do things his way."

Signs of John's ability with mathematics began to show when he was about 14. He read *Men of Mathematics* by E. T. Bell, and, inspired by its contents, he successfully carried out experiments and calculations described in it, and realized how much this type of complex work excited him—unlike the work given to him by his schoolteachers.

THE GIFTED MISFIT

By 1941, John had started at Bluefield College, Virginia. There he studied mathematics, science, and chemistry, and showed a real ability for problem-solving. He was also behaving more eccentrically. He had very few friends and his fellow students saw him as odd. John would play sinister pranks, drawing unflattering cartoons of pupils he disliked, and it was reported that he enjoyed inflicting pain on others, including animals—at one time he even tried to tie his sister Martha to a chair that was wired up with batteries. He didn't seem to have any sense that what he was doing was wrong.

At that time, a job as a mathematician was considered unusual, so while at Bluefield John thought he would probably go on to work in electrical engineering, as his father had. He still continued to conduct his elaborate and sometimes dangerous experiments—one of them involving explosives that accidentally led to the death of a pupil at his college.

On graduation from Bluefield College, John won a scholarship to the Carnegie Institute of Technology—now Carnegie-Mellon University—where he began studying in June 1945, at first for a degree in chemical engineering. His increasing interest in mathematics led him to take courses on calculus and relativity, which was when

he first came into contact with John Synge, the Head of Mathematics at the Carnegie Institute. Along with the other tutors there in the field, Synge quickly recognized John's extraordinary mathematical ability and persuaded him to transfer his main degree to that subject.

Though he was doing extremely well in his chosen studies, John did not deal well with failure on any level. When he entered a mathematics competition twice, and did not make the top five either time, he took it very badly. His tutors thought highly of him, but his fellow pupils at the Carnegie did not like him and made no secret of it. He was strong and big-built, which meant he wasn't physically bullied, but he was mocked by the other students, one of whom later said: "We tormented poor John. We were very unkind … We sensed he had a mental problem."

In 1948, John graduated from the Carnegie Institute, with a Bachelor of Arts and a Master's degree in mathematics, and though he was offered a place at several top universities, he decided to go to Princeton, where he could extend his qualifications in mathematics.

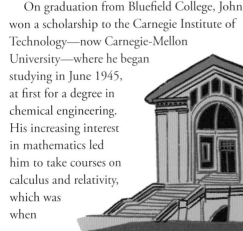

"YOU DON'T HAVE TO BE A MATHEMATICIAN TO HAVE A FEEL FOR NUMBERS."

SUCCESS AND SCHIZOPHRENIA

In September 1948, John was at Princeton University, where he showed an interest in a broad range of pure mathematics, including algebraic geometry and game theory—the science of strategy and decision-making. John avoided lectures, preferring to learn by himself and using his own methods to gain knowledge about the complex subjects he studied. This approach was frowned upon, but it was almost certainly what made him a highly original and creative mathematician who solved problems in ways no one else had considered. In 1950, John earned a doctorate degree from Princeton, and his accompanying thesis outlined what became known as the "Nash Equilibrium"—a highly important concept in game theory. Meanwhile his attitude once again prompted concern. He was described as odd, isolated, aloof, and "spooky."

Also in 1950, John embarked on a summer job working for RAND (a global policy "think tank") as a researcher into modern warfare for the US armed forces, which helped to sharpen its military strategies. When he returned to Princeton toward the end of that year, he applied for a permanent job at the university. Reportedly because of his off-putting personality, he was refused a place on the Princeton faculty. Instead, in 1951 he became part

"IT IS BETTER TO HAVE BEEN, THEN NOT TO HAVE BEEN, THEN TO HAVE BEEN NOTHING AT ALL."

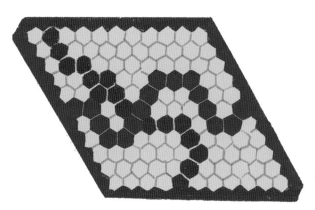

described as "among the most original results in geometric analysis of the twentieth century," and which would go on to earn him a Nobel Prize in 1994. By 1955, however, his mental health had noticeably deteriorated, and the schizophrenia he was to be later diagnosed with had started to take hold. He resigned from MIT in 1955. By this time, he had a child from a relationship with a woman called Eleanor Stier—though he went on to marry Alicia de Lardé, a Salvadoran-American physicist, in 1957.

Over the next few years, John's outstanding academic ability was gaining recognition in the wider world, and he would undoubtedly have won major scientific awards in the future, but by the early 1960s, John's severe mental illness had destroyed his career.

of the faculty of the Massachusetts Institute of Technology (MIT) where he conducted research into partial differential equations (equations that contain unknown and variable functions), which amongst other things are used to create computer models. The 1950s was the beginning of a decade in which John's landmark work in the field of game theory, and mathematics, some of which was

A BRILLIANT MIND

"IT IS ONLY IN THE MYSTERIOUS EQUATIONS OF LOVE THAT ANY LOGIC OR REASON CAN BE FOUND."

In 2015, John Nash Jr. was tragically killed in a car crash, along with his wife Alicia, shortly after returning from Norway to collect the Abel Prize for his contribution to the field of geometrical analysis. His life was not easy. He was a social and professional outcast for years, suffering with a frightening illness for much of his adult life. But with his great challenges he achieved a huge amount in the world of mathematical science, inspired many in his field, and produced theories that have been ultimately pivotal in preventing catastrophic wars.

John's work, particularly the Nash Equilibrium—a proposed solution of a game between two or more players in which each player is assumed to know the strategies of the other players—has been vital in the field of modern warfare, influencing the way military leaders have made their life-or-death decision making. Although he was a mathematician at his core, John Nash Jr.'s work on "game theory" has had wide-reaching implications for the scientific area of "quantitative theories" and beyond, changing the way we understand human psychology, global trade, and strategic forecasting. Leading geopolitical intelligence platforms have employed John's work

in game theory to better analyze the way leaders and states act, react, and make future decisions—and his work directly shaped the US and Soviet Cold War strategies in the 1960s and 1970s, where leaders used his concept to make and justify military decisions, such as not initiating nuclear attacks and thereby avoiding potential mass destruction.

After his release from a psychiatric hospital in 1962, and during a temporary separation from his wife Alicia, John Nash Jr. took to spending a lot of his time back in the halls of Princeton University, where he was said to be a ghost-like and fragile figure. But with the help of new treatments for schizophrenia, he continued to use his brilliant mathematical mind and produce work of outstanding quality. In 1994, John was jointly awarded with two others the Nobel Prize in Economics for his work on game theory. And in 1999, he received the Leroy P. Steele Prize from the American Mathematical Society. He has

fascinated not just scientists but also film-makers. The commercially successful movie *A Beautiful Mind*—a dramatic portrayal of John's troubled life and career—was released in 2002.

KATHERINE JOHNSON

BREAKING BARRIERS

Katherine Johnson was born Katherine Coleman on August 26, 1918, in White Sulphur Springs, West Virginia—the youngest of Joshua and Joylette Coleman's four children. Katherine's father Joshua mostly worked as a handyman at a local hotel, while her mother Joylette was a teacher.

From an early age, Katherine was a top student in school—with a particular gift for mathematics. Her strong curiosity and natural ability with numbers meant she advanced much more quickly than the other pupils her age, and by the time she was 10 years old she had completed the eighth grade (her classmates were 13 or 14). At that time, African-Americans in her town were not offered the same educational opportunities as the white community, and Katherine's schooling might have ended at that point had her father Joshua not made the decision to move the family 190 km (120 miles) away to West Virginia, where a school accepted Katherine and she could continue her studies.

At 13 years old, Katherine had started high school on the same campus—or grounds—as the West Virginia State College. At high school, she continued to excel at her subjects and particularly the sciences. After she graduated, she applied for a degree course at the West Virginia State College and was accepted, embarking on the study of mathematics at the age of 18. It was at WVSC that she found a couple of influential tutors: Dr. Angie King, and the man who was to become her mentor, Professor W.W. Schieffelin Claytor—who himself had been the third-ever African-American to earn a Ph.D. in mathematics. Under Claytor's guidance and through her own hard work, Katherine graduated from the college in 1937 with the highest possible score in her degree in Mathematics and French. Shortly afterward, she took a job teaching at a black public school in Marion, Virginia. It was around this time that she met and married her husband, James Francis Goble.

THE HUMAN COMPUTER

Though she was doing very well in her job in Marion, Katherine's education was not over yet. In 1938, Virginia's president, Dr. John W. Davis, selected Katherine and two male students for places at West Virginia University, the state's flagship graduate school, making her one of the first three black students to be given this opportunity. Katherine then left her teaching job and embarked on the graduate mathematics course at the university. By this time, though, she and her husband had decided they wanted to have children—and sooner rather than later—and at the end of her first term, Katherine left WVU to start a family with James. She didn't go back to continue her education for 14 years.

As soon as she considered her three children old enough, Katherine returned to work as a schoolteacher. It wasn't until 1952 that she found out about open positions at West Area Computing, part of the National Advisory Committee for Aeronautics (NACA). Katherine learned that WCA was hiring African-American women to serve as "computers"—meaning people who performed and checked calculations for technological developments. Intrigued, she applied for a role there, and the following year she was accepted for a position at Langley Research Center in Hampton, Virginia, at the laboratory run by scientist Dorothy Vaughan.

Katherine and James moved with their children so that she could take up her role in the Langley

Laboratory where she was assigned to a temporary role on a project in the Flight Research Division. Her excellent work meant she was soon offered a full-time position and she spent fours years examining data from flight tests, analyzing material from a plane crash caused by turbulence in mid-air.

Katherine's forthright nature and natural scientific curiosity meant she was sometimes a little frustrated by the lack of ambition of many her female colleagues. She later said of her role at the laboratory: "The women did what they were told to do … They didn't ask questions or take the task any further. I asked questions; I wanted to know why." At this time, the environment she worked in was made difficult by racism and the Federal Workplace Segregation Laws, which meant that African-Americans were required to work and eat separately from white Americans, and use different toilet facilities to their white counterparts.

It was while she working at the laboratory that her husband became seriously ill, and he died from cancer just as her work there was finishing.

GET THE GIRL

In 1957, the launch of the Soviet satellite *Sputnik 1* not only changed history, it changed Katherine Johnson's life. That year, she worked on some of the vital mathematical calculations that would contribute to a 1958 document called "Notes on Space Technology." This document also contained a collection of lectures given by engineers who together formed the Space Task Group behind NACA's first official venture into space travel. Since she had worked with many of the engineers throughout her time at the Langley Laboratory, Katherine was invited to become part of the project. NACA was dismantled that year and became what we now know as NASA. As part of this new team, Katherine worked on analysis for America's first human flight into space and in 1960, she and an engineer called Ted Skopinski wrote a report together that set out the mathematical equations for an orbital spaceflight so that the landing position of the spacecraft was accurately predicted. Katherine's work on this document made her the first woman in the Flight Research Division to be given credit as co-author of a research report.

It was in 1962 that Katherine was asked to perform the work for which she would become most recognized. That year, NASA was preparing for the orbital flight of astronaut John Glenn—and the complex nature of the flight required background preparation of the highest accuracy, linking computers and flight tracking stations around the world in places such as Washington, DC, Cape Canaveral, and Bermuda. The computers containing vital calculations were prone to blackouts, however, and the astronauts heading the flight mission worried about putting all their faith in a machine. Her reputation as a highly skilled mathematical calculator was such that John Glenn himself sent out a message to engineers to "get the girl"—meaning, make sure that Katherine Johnson runs the same numbers contained in the computers, but by hand on her desktop calculating machine. Katherine proudly recalled the moment Glenn said, "I'm ready to go," and his successful flight became a game-changer in the fierce competition between the United States and the Soviet Union.

Along with this first incredible contribution to the space race, Katherine found the time to go on and author or co-author 26 more research reports.

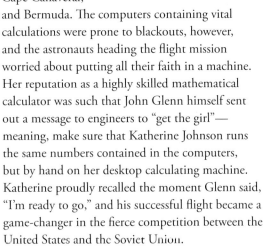

"WE WILL ALWAYS HAVE STEM WITH US. SOME THINGS WILL DROP OUT OF THE PUBLIC EYE AND WILL GO AWAY, BUT THERE WILL ALWAYS BE SCIENCE, ENGINEERING, AND TECHNOLOGY. AND THERE WILL ALWAYS, ALWAYS BE MATHEMATICS."

HIDDEN FIGURES

"LIKE WHAT YOU DO, AND THEN YOU WILL DO YOUR BEST."

Katherine Johnson's calculations of "orbital mechanics" as a NASA employee were critical to the success of the first ever and subsequent US flights into space. During her 35-year career both at NASA and the National Advisory Committee for Aeronautics, she earned a reputation for mastering complex manual calculations and helped the space agency pioneer the use of computers to perform the tasks. She did vital work on calculating flight paths, launch windows, and emergency return paths for Project Mercury spaceflights, including those for astronauts Alan Shepard, the first American in space, and John Glenn, the first American in orbit—along with what are known as "rendezvous paths" for the Apollo Lunar Module and command module on flights to the Moon.

With growing advances in computers, Katherine adapted quickly to new technology and used it to great effect when calculating the flight path of the *Apollo 11*, which landed on the moon in 1969. In 1970, her work was again vital in the *Apollo 13* moon mission. Though that mission was terminated shortly after take-off, it was Katherine's careful preparations and back-up procedures that meant the disappointed crew's landing back on Earth was safe. Her devised systems are a blueprint for modern spaceflight safety and efficiency.

Toward the end of her working life, Katherine worked on the Space Shuttle, the Earth Resources Satellite, and a mission to Mars. Though she retired in 1986, at the age of 68, after 33 years at the Langley Laboratory, she said, "I loved going to work every single day."

In 2015, at 97 years old, Katherine was awarded the Presidential Medal of Freedom—America's highest civilian award— by US president Barack Obama for her services to the country. Her life's work was charted, along with the work of some of her fellow mathematicians, in the book *Hidden Figures* by Margot Lee Shetterly, which in 2016 was made into a movie of the same name. Katherine proudly attended the movie premiere. She died at the age of 101 in 2020.

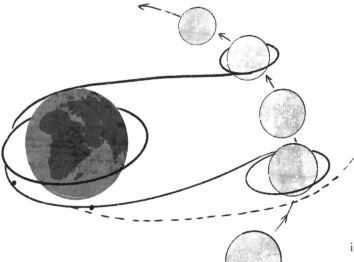

RITA LEVI-MONTALCINI

STRIVING FOR AN EDUCATION

Rita Levi-Montalcini was born with her twin sister Paola, on April 22, 1909, in Turin, Italy. They were the youngest of four children, and their two older siblings were Gino and Anna. Rita's parents were Sephardic Jews. Her father, Adamo Levi, was an electrical engineer and mathematician and her mother, Adele Montalcini, was a painter.

Rita's early childhood was happy and her family were close. She looked up to her older sister Anna, who was passionate about literature, and as a young teenager Rita dreamed of becoming a writer. Her parents were highly cultured and encouraged an appreciation of art and intellect in all their children—though their values were quite traditional. Her father admired and respected women, but he believed their place was in the home looking after the family, not at study or pursuing a career. Initially, Adamo made the decision that none of his three daughters needed to be educated to university or degree level, and only his son Gino should embark on further education.

While her twin sister Paola showed early talent as a painter and was encouraged to continue with this, Rita, who was not particularly creative in that way, was a little frustrated. She knew from an early age that she did not want to conform to the conventional idea of what a woman should be or do, and by this time she realized she was interested in the sciences, like her father Adamo. She pleaded with him to let her study for a career and eventually he agreed. Rita then wasted no time in learning Latin, Greek, and mathematics at high school. After witnessing a family friend die from stomach cancer, she made up her mind that she wanted to work in medicine and was determined to achieve her ambition. At high school she worked very hard on languages and in all the sciences, earning excellent marks in her final exams. This meant she was accepted on graduation in the late 1920s to begin a degree course in medicine at Turin University.

THWARTED BY WAR

"IF I HAD NOT BEEN DISCRIMINATED AGAINST OR HAD NOT SUFFERED PERSECUTION, I WOULD NEVER HAVE RECEIVED THE NOBEL PRIZE."

At Turin university, Rita studied under the Italian neurohistologist, Giuseppe Levi, who was a great influence on her. She later talked about how much she owed him for his superb training in biological science and his particular approach to solving complex problems. In 1936, Rita graduated from Turin with a degree in Medicine and Surgery, though she remained at the university as Guiseppe Levi's assistant, working in neurology and psychiatry.

It was after Benito Mussolini came to power in Italy in the late 1930s that Rita's academic career was abruptly cut short. In 1938, a state law preventing Jews from holding university positions was passed and Rita was forced to leave her role at Turin. Determined to continue the work she'd started, she spent some time in Belgium, at a neurological institute, before returning to Italy in the spring of 1940, just as World War II was beginning in earnest. Though Rita's Jewish family were under threat from the invasion of the Germany army, they refused to leave their home in Turin; instead they stayed and kept a low profile. Rita meanwhile built herself her own scientific laboratory in her bedroom. Here,

she studied the growth of nerve threads in chicken embryos—and this formed the foundations of her later, vital work and medical research.

In 1941, heavy bombing in Turin meant that Rita was forced to leave the city and move out to Piedmont in the countryside, where she carefully rebuilt her laboratory and continued with the experiments she had begun. In 1943, when bombing spread out to where she was living, Rita moved again, this time to Florence. In August 1944, the Allied armies forced the Nazi army to leave Florence and Rita was hired as a medical doctor, and was quickly assigned to a refugee camp in the city. Here, hundreds of refugees were being sent from the North of Italy, where the war was still going on. At the camp, Rita saw a lot of suffering. Many of the refugees were badly infected with diseases such as typhus and though she tried, Rita was unable to save a lot of them from dying.

When World War II ended in 1945, Rita finally returned to Turin and her position at the university. Then, two years later, she received the invitation that would change her life …

THE WAR ON CANCER

In 1947, Rita was contacted by the American professor Viktor Hamburger, who worked at Washington University in St. Louis. Professor Hamburger had heard of the experiments on chick embryos that Rita had started in her bedroom years before, which mirrored his own—and he asked her if she would come and work in his laboratory in Washington. Rita agreed, planning to stay in Washington for just a short time, but the great results of her work under Viktor Hamburger meant he offered her the position of Associate Professor at the university where she could focus on research, and she accepted.

It was at Washington University in 1952 that Rita did her most important work contributing to cancer research, based around "nerve growth factor"—when she observed the fast growth of nerve cells from certain cancerous tissues. In her experiments, Rita placed samples of cancerous matter into chick embryos, and saw the speed with which nerve threads grew around the matter—like a kind of halo. This suggested to Rita that the mass of cancerous cells was releasing something was making the nerves grow. This gave her and medical science a startling insight into how cancer behaves in the body, and so potentially how it could be managed and treated.

In 1958, Rita accepted the role of full Professor at Washington University, and four years later in 1962, she also set up the Research Center of Neurobiology in Rome—splitting her time between there and St. Louis. In 1963, because of her vital research into neurological conditions, Rita was given the prestigious Max Weinstein Award by the United Cerebral Palsy Association—and in 1969, she became Director of the Institute of Cell Biology in Rome. In the 1970s, she worked with the Italian Pharmaceutical Industry, testing drugs for use in neurological conditions.

Though she officially retired in the late 1970s, Rita stayed on as Guest Professor at the Institute of Cell Biology in Rome and continued to make important advances in medical science. In 1986, due to her work with the scientist Stanley Cohen on research into Nerve Growth Factor—or NGF—she was awarded the Nobel Prize in medicine jointly with Cohen. And in 1990, Rita was one of the first scientists to highlight the importance of the mast cell—a cell found in human tissue that protects the body against allergic reactions. By 2002, Rita had established the European Brain Research Institute.

"THE MOST IMPORTANT PART OF OUR BRAIN, THAT WHICH IS NEOCORTICAL, MUST BE USED TO HELP OTHERS AND NOT JUST TO MAKE DISCOVERIES."

ACCOLADES

Rita Levi-Montalcini died in Rome on December 30, 2012, at the age of 103. In a life devoted to her career, she never married and had no children. A few years before her death she said, "My life has been enriched by excellent human relations, work, and interests. I have never felt lonely." She received many tributes, including one from the Vatican in Rome which rightly described her as an "inspiring example for Italy and the world."

Her work gave science profound insights into how the nervous system regulates the number and growth of cells during its development, and opened up hopeful avenues of research into cancer, embryology, nerve regeneration, and neurodegenerative diseases (progressive brain diseases) that continue to this day.

Rita's great achievements are made even more impressive by her early encounters with sexism and anti-Semitism as a young woman—and her tireless work with the wounded and suffering Jewish refugees during World War II. Right to the end of her long life, she never stopped working—or fighting what she saw as injustice. In 1991, after being given the "Laurea Honoris Causa" award from the University of Trieste in Italy, she became active in human rights in her native country and successfully campaigned for the Trieste Declaration of Human Duties. In August 2001, she became more involved in Italian politics and was made a Senator for Life by the then president of Italy, Carlo Azeglio Ciampi.

In her lifetime, Rita received many awards and accolades. In 1986, she shared with Stanley Cohen the Nobel Prize for Medicine for her discovery of Nerve Growth Factor, and in 1968, she became the tenth woman to be elected to the United States National Academy of Sciences. In 1986, she shared with Stanley Cohen the Nobel Prize for Medicine, and a year later she received the US National Medal of Science—the nation's highest scientific award. In 1996, Rita became a Fellow of the American Academy of Arts and Sciences.

"ABOVE ALL, DON'T FEAR DIFFICULT MOMENTS. THE BEST COMES FROM THEM."

GLOSSARY

Algebra
Algebra is an area of mathematics that uses letters and symbols to represent numbers and other quantities. It includes problem solving, patterns, and reasoning.

Anthropology
The study of human cultures and the development of societies.

Arithmetic
Arithmetic is an area of mathematics that works with numbers using addition, subtraction, multiplication and division. For example, 3 + 3 = 6, and 10 x 2 = 20.

Asperger Syndrome
A form of autism. A lifelong condition that makes people experience the world

differently. People with autism sometimes struggle with social situations, and can find it difficult to understand others' thoughts and feelings.

Astronomy
A branch of science that examines the Universe as a whole and the space objects within it.

Astrophysics
A branch of science that examines the Universe as a whole and the space objects within it.

Autism
A lifelong condition that makes people to experience the world differently. People with autism sometimes struggle with social situations, and find it difficult to understand others' thoughts and feelings.

Big Bang Theory
The Big Bang Theory is the most widely recognized theory about how the Universe began. It states that it started as a very small singularity which has since expanded, and continues to expand.

Cosmology
Cosmology is the scientific study of the development of the Universe, which includes the Big Bang theory.

Cosmonaut
A cosmonaut is a person who has been trained by the Russian Space Agency to work in space; a Russian astronaut.

Crystallography
The science that looks specifically at the arrangement of atoms in crystals and examines their structures.

DNA
Deoxyribonucleic acid (DNA) is the material found in every cell in a human (and most other organisms). It is responsible for passing on physical traits from one generation to the next.

Electromagnetic radiation
In physics, electromagnetic radiation refers to the waves that travel through space, which carry energy. Electromagnetic radiation includes radio waves, X-rays, microwaves, and light.

Ethnology
Ethnology is the study of different peoples characteristics, and their relationships to each other.

Geology
This is the science that looks at the structure, features, and materials of Earth.

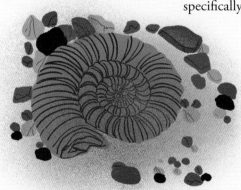

Heliocentrism
An astrological model that demonstrates the Sun is at the very middle of our solar system.

Neuroscientist
A scientist that studies the human nervous system and brain.

Nuclear physics
Nuclear physics is the study of protons and neutrons, which are found at the core of an atom. It is used in the development of nuclear power, medicine, and weapons.

Palaeontology
The study of the history of life based on fossilized remains of animals, plants, fungi, and bacteria.

Paleobotany
The study of fossilized plants, specifically.

Physicist
A scientist that specializes in physics, which is concerned with energy and matter, including heat, light, sound, electricity, and magnetism

Psychologist
An expert in the study of the human mind and actions.

Radiotherapy
A form of medical treatment that uses X-rays or other radiation to treat illnesses such as cancer.

Theory of relativity
The theory that space and time are relative—not absolute.

Zoology
The scientific study of animals; their actions, physical structure, and classification.

INDEX